AN EXORCIST TELLS HIS STORY

FATHER GABRIELE AMORTH

An Exorcist Tells His Story

Translated by Nicoletta V. MacKenzie

IGNATIUS PRESS   SAN FRANCISCO

Title of the Italian original:
Un escorista raconta
© 1990 Edizioni Dehoniane, Rome

Cover art:
Expulsion of the Devils from Arezzo, Story of St. Francis, detail
Giotto di Bondone
Upper Church, S. Francesco, Assisi, Italy
Scala/Art Resource, NY

Cover design by Roxanne Mei Lum

CONTENTS

FOREWORD
TO THE AMERICAN EDITION

When asked, as a psychologist involved in things spiritual, to introduce this edition, at first I declined. Although I have had experience with those suffering from what I am convinced were diabolical influences, I have difficulties with Fr. Amroth's approach. He writes of this intriguing subject in ways quite foreign to the ideas of the English-speaking world, a world that vacillates between severe rationalism and wild speculation. The behavioral sciences are divided on the existence and nature of paranormal phenomena, as the highly respected Professor Benjamin Wolman has noted in *The Handbook of Parapsychology*, a standard work.

Although Fr. Amorth is by no means naïve about the psychological causes of aberrant behavior, his own work as an exorcist is not a form of psychotherapy. It is a spiritual ministry. He has been very successful in helping a wide range of persons with acute disturbances quite beyond the scope of clinical diagnosis. He raises the issue of the diabolical, which almost always gets a response of ill-informed prejudice. He makes us think.

As a priest rather than a clinician, I recognize in this book the account of an intelligent and dedicated pastor of souls who has had the courage to go where most of us fear to tread. He uses a rhetoric foreign to most of us and even theological concepts alien to our way of thinking. But the same can be said of the Gospel accounts of our Savior's

7

own work when delivering "those possessed by evil spirits". This book needs to be read with care but with an open mind.

Father Benedict J. Groeschel, C.F.R., Ed.D.

FOREWORD
TO THE ITALIAN EDITION

It is with great pleasure that I write a few words to introduce Father Gabriele Amorth's book. Father Amorth has
been my worthy collaborator for many years in the ministry of exorcist. He and I have experienced together some of
the events reported in this book, and together we have
shared the worries, hardships, and hopes of helping the
many suffering people who have turned to us.

It is also with pleasure that I welcome the publication of
these pages, because, although in these last decades much
has been written in almost every field of Catholic morality
and theology, the topic of exorcism has been all but forgotten. Maybe it is because of this lack of study and interest
that, even now, the only part of the *Ritual* that has not been
updated according to the postconciliar directives of the
Second Vatican Council is the one concerning exorcisms.
Despite this, the importance of the ministry to "expel demons" is great, as we can see from the Gospels, from the
actions of the apostles, and from the history of the Church.

When Saint Peter, by supernatural inspiration, was led
to the house of Cornelius the centurion to announce the
Christian faith to the first handful of gentiles, he demonstrated that God was truly with Jesus by stressing in a concrete way his ability to free all who were in the grip of the
devil (Acts 10:1–38). The Gospels often show the extraordinary powers that Jesus possessed over evil with concrete
examples. By expelling demons, our Lord could not have

chosen a more powerful way to show us that the Father sent his only begotten Son into this world to put an end to the dark reign of Satan over men.

Sacred Scripture assures us that the forms of Satan's power over the world include physical obsession. Jesus repeatedly stressed the ability to expel demons among the specific powers that he wanted to pass on to his apostles and their successors (Mt 10:8; Mk 3:5; Lk 9:1).

Although God allows some people to experience diabolical oppression, he provides several means of powerful aid for them. God not only gave his Church many effective sacramental powers to help her cope against Satan's deadly activities; since the beginning, he also chose the Most Holy Virgin Mary as a permanent antidote to the enmity between mankind and Satan (see Candido Amantini, *Il mistero di Maria* [Naples: Dehoniane, 1971]).

The majority of contemporary writers—Catholic theologians included—do not deny the existence of Satan and the other rebellious angels but discount the extent of their influence upon human affairs. Indeed, in many quarters to discredit physical diabolical influence is considered a duty and proof of wisdom. Contemporary culture as a whole believes that to credit anything other than natural factors for events and occurrences all around us is an old-fashioned illusion.

It is obvious that this belief greatly helps the work of the evil one, especially as it is shared by those who are entrusted with the task and the power to hinder his foul activities. If instead of following contemporary culture we followed Sacred Scripture, theology, and daily experience, we would be convinced that there are great numbers of unhappy people who are possessed by demons and that science can offer them very little help indeed. In the majority of instances, those who are able to recognize the symptoms that are commonly associated with demonic activity can prudently diagnose a case of "demonopathy"—this is the term for every diabolical influence.

An illness that is associated with even the lowest levels of demonic activity is peculiarly resistant to every known prescription drug. In contrast, even illnesses that are considered mortal are mysteriously healed by religious interventions. Often the victims of an evil spirit believe that they are persecuted by bad luck: they see their life as a series of misfortunes.

Today, science admits that some behavior is caused by abnormal factors and calls "paranormal" all inexplicable actions performed by those possessed by demons. Many people are seeking to find the causes of these phenomena. We do not try to deny scientific progress; we merely state that we deny reality if we delude ourselves that science can explain everything and that we can trace every illness to normal activities.

Very few scientists seriously believe in the possibility that unknown, intelligent, and incorporeal powers can cause certain phenomena. Rare is the doctor who will admit that he may be dealing with a different set of causes when faced with patients whose symptoms and clinical tests are unexplainable. If they are confronted with the unexplainable, many people will appeal to Freud rather than call an exorcist to help. As a result, the condition of these unfortunate patients does not improve but becomes worse.

Father Amorth's brief and clear book allows the reader to witness the activities of the exorcist. These pages do not attempt to explain the theory of the existence of demons and of demonic possession or to reach doctrinal conclusions. They merely let the facts speak for themselves by allowing the reader to experience what an exorcist sees and does. I know how much the author loves the priests of the Church who have been entrusted by Christ with the power to expel demons in his name. I am confident that this book will be beneficial to many of them and that it may inspire others to write about their experiences on the same subject.

Father Candido Amantini

AUTHOR'S INTRODUCTION

When the Pope's Vicar for the Diocese of Rome, Cardinal Ugo Poletti, unexpectedly granted me the faculty of exorcist, I did not guess the immensity of the world that he had opened up to me or the multitudes who would flock to my ministry.

I was initially assigned as assistant to Father Candido Amantini, a Passionist priest, who was a renowned and expert exorcist. Those in need of his help would come from all parts of Italy, and often from abroad, to his headquarters, the church of the Holy Staircase in Rome. This assignment was a great grace to me; I believe that Father Candido was the only person in the world who could claim an experience of thirty-six years as a full-time exorcist. I could not have had a better teacher, and I thank him for the infinite patience with which he introduced me to this ministry.

I discovered something else. There are very few exorcists in Italy, even fewer who are well prepared, and fewer still in other countries. Therefore, I found myself blessing people from France, Austria, Germany, Switzerland, Spain, and England, because—those who came to me assured me—they had not been able to find an exorcist. Was it because bishops and priests did not care? Or was it because they honestly did not believe in the necessity and efficacy of this ministry? Whatever the reason, I felt I had been called to an apostolate among people who suffered greatly and whom nobody understood—neither their relatives, nor their doctors, nor their priests.

While this pastoral ministry is entirely overlooked in the Catholic world today, it was not so in the past. In some denominations of the Protestant church, exorcisms are still practiced frequently and fruitfully. Each cathedral should have an exorcist, just as it has a "penitentiary". Where there is a greater need—such as in large parishes and in sanctuaries—there should also be a greater number of exorcists.

Not only are exorcists few in number, but also they are barely tolerated, and at times they are hindered. They seldom find anyone willing to open his door to them. Everyone knows that sometimes people possessed by demons scream; this is the main reason why a pastor or the superior of a religious order does not want an exorcist on his property. Peace and quiet become more important than the charity of healing people who are possessed. Even I have experienced this hostility, although less so than others who are better and more renowned exorcists. First of all, I would like to alert bishops of the gravity of the problem. Bishops must realize that this ministry is entirely entrusted to their care: it is only they who can practice or delegate an exorcism. Sadly, since most bishops have never performed an exorcism, they are seldom aware of the extent of the need.

This book was prompted by my desire to share the knowledge acquired through much experience, mainly Father Candido's, with people who are interested in this topic. Primarily I wish to be of service to other exorcists and priests. Just as every general practitioner must be able to refer his patients to the most appropriate specialist (for example, ear, nose, and throat specialist; orthopedic surgeon; or neurologist), so must a priest be able to determine when someone needs an exorcist. In fact, many priests encouraged me to write this book because one of the guidelines of the *Ritual* for exorcisms recommends that exorcists study "many useful documents written by experts".

However, when we try to find serious books on this topic, we find that very little is available. I will recommend the following three books: *Il diavolo* by Monsignor Balducci (Piemme, 1988); its historical section is useful, but not the practical section. This book is limited in scope and contains numerous errors; the author is an expert in demonology, not in exorcisms. *La preghiera di liberazione* (Palermo: Herbita, 1985) by Father Matteo La Grua, who is an exorcist, was written for the renewal groups, and its intent is to guide their prayers of deliverance. *Cronista all'inferno* by Renzo Allegri (Mondadori, 1990) is also worth mentioning. This volume is not a methodical research but a collection of reputable interviews. It presents extreme cases, the most sensational situations, which, while true, do not represent the normal daily workload of the exorcist.

In conclusion: I have striven in these pages to fill a void and to present the argument from every angle, although concisely, in order to reach a greater number of readers. I intend to write further in other books, and I hope that others write with competence and religious sensitivity, so that the topic can be treated with the proper depth, which was found in times past among Catholics but is now found only among Protestants.

I want to make it clear that I will not attempt to demonstrate truths that are thoroughly discussed in other publications, such as the existence of demons, the reality of demonic possession, and the power to expel demons, which Christ gave to those who believe in the Gospel message. These are all revealed truths; they are found in the Bible; they have been thoroughly covered in theology; and they are constantly taught by the Magisterium of the

Church. I choose instead to dwell on what is less known and on practical aspects that may be useful to exorcists and to anyone who wishes to learn about the subject. I apologize for repeating some fundamental concepts.

May the Immaculate Virgin—who was an enemy of Satan from the announcement of salvation (Gen 3:15) until its fulfillment (Rev 12) and who is united to her Son in the battle to defeat him—bless this work of mine. It is the fruit of an exhausting activity that I pursue with confidence, trusting in her maternal protection.

The following notes are added to the latest, expanded edition of this book. I did not expect the success that this volume encountered or the many reprints that followed in a short period of time. This success merely confirms my opinion that there is a great deal of interest in the topic of exorcism and that in Italy and in the entire Catholic world there were no other Catholic books that thoroughly—even if briefly—addressed exorcisms. This fact is significant and painful. It indicates what is an inexplicable lack of interest or maybe what is simply a real lack of belief on the part of those who should be leading the research.

I thank everyone who has supported and praised me, especially other exorcists. The most welcome approval came from my mentor, Father Candido Amantini, who recognized his teachings in my book. The criticisms I received were few and minor; therefore, I did not make any corrections, nor did I see any need to modify the book. I merely expanded some areas to give a more complete picture of the topic. I also believe that those people and groups whom I took to task understood my good intentions and did not take offense. I have used the printed media in an effort to serve a larger number of people. It is the same zeal that prompts me to serve all those who daily seek my ministry of exorcist.

I thank the Lord for everything. I must add the following comment to the tenth Italian edition (1993) of this book. Something has changed in the two years since my book first appeared. Bishops have written important documents, the number of exorcists has increased, some bishops are now performing exorcisms, and new books on the subject have been added to mine. Something is moving. I do not claim the merit; I am simply reporting the facts.

I cannot conclude without a fond remembrance of Father Candido Amantini, whom the Lord called to his reward on September 22, 1992. It was the day of Saint Candido, Father Amantini's patron saint. To his brother priests who came to wish him well, he simply answered, "Today I asked Saint Candido for a gift."

Father Candido was born in 1914. At sixteen years of age he joined the Passionist Fathers. He was a professor of Sacred Scripture and morality. He performed his greatest service, that of exorcist, for thirty-six years. He would see from sixty to eighty people every morning and masked his tiredness behind a smiling face. Many times his advice was inspired. Padre Pio said of him, "Father Candido is a priest according to God's heart."

This book, with the exceptions of my own mistakes, is intended as a testimonial to Father Candido's experience as an exorcist, for the benefit of all those who are interested in the subject. Since this testimonial is one of the main reasons for this book, it pleased me greatly when he acknowledged that my writings were faithful to his teachings.

THE CENTRALITY OF CHRIST

The devil is one of God's creatures. We cannot talk about him and about exorcisms without first stating some basic facts about God's plan for creation. We will not say anything new, but we might present a new perspective.

All too often we have the wrong concept of creation, and we take for granted the following wrong sequence of events. We believe that one day God created the angels; that he put them to the test, although we are not sure which test; and that as a result we have the division among angels and demons. The angels were rewarded with heaven, and the demons were punished with hell. Then we believe that on another day God created the universe, the minerals, the plants, the animals, and, in the end, man. In the Garden of Eden, Adam and Eve obeyed Satan and disobeyed God; thus they sinned. At this point, to save mankind, God decided to send his Son.

This is not what the Bible teaches us, and it is not the teaching of the Fathers. If this were so, the angels and creation would remain strangers to the mystery of Christ. If we read the prologue to the Gospel of John and the two christological hymns that open the Letters to the Ephesians and the Colossians, we see that Christ is "the firstborn of all creatures" (Col 1:15). Everything was created for him and in the expectation of him. There is no theological discussion that makes any sense if it asks whether Christ would have been born without the sin of Adam. Christ is the center of creation; all creatures, both heavenly (the angels) and earthly (men) find in him their summation. On the other hand, we can affirm that, given the sin of our forebears, Christ's coming assumed a particular role: he came as Savior. The core of his action is contained within the Paschal mystery: through the blood of his Cross, he reconciles all things in the heavens (angels) and on earth (men) to God. The role of every creature is dependent on this christocentric understanding.

We cannot omit a reflection about the Virgin Mary. If the firstborn creature is the Word become flesh, she who would be the means of the Incarnation must also have been present in the divine thought before every other creature. From this stems Mary's unique relationship with the Holy Trinity.

We must also mention the influence that Christ has on angels and demons. Concerning angels, some theologians believe that the angels were admitted to the beatific vision of God only by virtue of the mystery of the Cross. Many Fathers also make interesting statements. For instance, Saint Athanasius writes that the angels owe their salvation to the blood of Christ. The Gospels give us many statements concerning demons, and they clearly state that Christ defeated the reign of Satan with his Cross and established the reign of God. The demons who possessed the Gerasene man exclaimed, "What is there between us, Son of God? Have you come to torment us before our time?" (Mt 8:29). This is an obvious reference to the fact that the power of Satan is gradually broken by Christ. Satan's power, therefore, still exists and will continue to exist until our salvation will be completed, "because the accuser of our brethren will be cast out" (Rev 12:10). Additional information on the role of Mary, enemy of Satan since the original announcement of salvation, can be found in the beautiful book by Father Candido Amantini, *Il mistero di Maria* (Naples: Dehoniane, 1971).

If we see everything in the light of the centrality of Christ, we can see God's plan, who created everything "for him and in expectation of him". And we can see the actions of Satan, the enemy, the tempter, the accuser. By means of his temptation, evil, pain, sin, and death entered the world. It is in this context that we are able to see the restoration of God's plan, which Christ accomplished at the cost of his blood.

In this context, we are made aware of the power of the devil. Jesus calls him "the prince of this world" (Jn 12:31, 14:30, 16:11). John affirms that "the whole world is in the power of the evil one" (1 Jn 5:19); by "the world" John means everything that is opposed to God. Satan was the brightest of the angels; he became the most evil of the devils and their chief. The demons remain bound to the same strict hierarchy that was given them when they were angels: principalities, thrones, dominions, and so on (Col 1:16). However, while the angels, whose chief is Michael, are bound by a hierarchy of love, the demons live under a rule of slavery.

We are also made aware of the action of Christ, who shattered the reign of Satan and established the kingdom of God. This is why the instances where Jesus freed those possessed by demons become particularly important. When Peter teaches Cornelius about Christ, he does not mention any miracle besides the fact that he cured "all those who had fallen under the power of the devil" (Acts 10:38). We understand, then, why the first authority that Jesus gave his apostles was the power to expel demons (Mt 10:1). We can make the same statement for all believers: "These are the signs that will be associated with believers:

in my name they will cast out devils" (Mk 16:17). Thus Jesus heals and reestablishes the divine plan that had been ruined by the rebellion of some of the angels and by our forefathers.

We must make this abundantly clear: evil, suffering, death, and hell (that is, eternal damnation in everlasting torment) *are not acts of God*. I want to expand on this point. One day Father Candido was expelling a demon. Toward the end of the exorcism, he turned to the evil spirit and sarcastically told him, "Get out of here. The Lord has already prepared a nice, well-heated house for you!" At this, the demon answered, "You do not know anything! It wasn't he [God] who made hell. It was us. He had not even thought about it." Similarly, on another occasion, while I was questioning a demon to know whether he had contributed to the creation of hell, I received this answer: "All of us cooperated."

Christ's centrality in the plan of creation, and its restoration through redemption, is fundamental to understanding God's plan and the end of the world. Angels and men received an intelligent and free nature. When I am told (by those who confuse predestination with God's providence) that God already knows who will be saved and who will be damned, and therefore anything we do is useless, I usually answer with four truths that the Bible spells out for us: God wants that everyone be saved; no one is predestined to go to hell; Jesus died for everyone; and everyone is given sufficient graces for salvation.

Christ's centrality tells us that we can be saved only in his name. It is only in his name that we can win and free ourselves from the enemy of our salvation, Satan. At the end of the most difficult exorcisms, when I am confronted with total demonic possession, I pray the christological hymn of the Letter of Paul to the Philippians (2:6–11). When I speak the words "so that all beings in the heavens, on earth, and in the underworld should bend the knee at the name of Jesus", I kneel, everyone present kneels, and always the one possessed by the demons is also compelled to kneel. It is a moving and powerful moment. I always feel that all the legions of the angels are surrounding us, kneeling at the name of Jesus.

THE POWER OF SATAN

Because of the subject that I have decided to address in this book, I cannot pursue other very interesting theological questions. I will merely touch upon certain points that come up as a result of exorcisms. An exorcist with a solid theological and scriptural background, such as Father Candido, who spoke with demons for thirty-six years, is well qualified to make some assumptions on subjects—such as the sin of the rebellious angels—that theologians have dismissed in the past with a "we do not know". Everything that God created follows a harmonious design; therefore, the smallest atom influences everything, and every shadow casts some darkness on everything. Theology will be unfinished and incomprehensible until it focuses on the world of the angels. A Christology that ignores Satan is crippled and will never understand the magnitude of redemption.

We will now continue with Christ, the center of the universe. Everything was created for him and in view of his Coming, in the heavens (angels) and on earth (the tangible world, man first of all). It would be wonderful to speak only of Christ, but it would not be according to his every teaching and action, and we would never be able to understand him. Scripture talks to us about the kingdom of God but also of the kingdom of Satan. It tells us about the power of God, the Creator and Lord of the universe, but also of the power of darkness. It speaks of the sons of God and of the sons of Satan. It is impossible to understand the salvific

action of Christ if we ignore the destructive action of
Satan.

Satan was the most perfect being created by the hands of
God. His God-given authority and superiority over the
other angels are recognized by all, so he thought that he had
the same authority over everything that God was creating.
Satan tried to understand all of creation but could not,
because all the plan of creation was oriented toward Christ.
Until Christ came into the world, God's plan could not be
revealed in its entirety. Hence Satan's rebellion. He wanted
to continue to be the absolute first, the center of creation,
even if it meant opposing God's design. This is why Satan
continually tries to dominate the world ("the whole world
is in the power of the evil one", 1 Jn 5:19). Beginning with
our forefathers, he seeks to enslave men by making them
obey himself and disobey God. He was successful with our
forefathers, Adam and Eve, and he hoped to continue with
all men with the help of "a third of the angels", who, according to the book of Revelation, followed him in rebellion against God.

God never rejects his creatures. Therefore, even though
they broke with God, Satan and his angels maintain their
power and rank (thrones, dominions, principalities, powers, and so on) even if they use them for evil purposes. Saint
Augustine does not exaggerate when he claims that, if God
gave Satan a free hand, "no man would be left alive." Since
Satan cannot kill us, he tries to "make us into his followers
in opposition to God, just as he is in opposition to God".

The truth of salvation is this: Jesus came "to destroy the
works of the devil" (1 Jn 3:8), to free man from Satan's
slavery, and to establish the kingdom of God after destroying the reign of Satan. However, between the first coming
of Christ and the Parousia (the second, triumphal coming

of Christ as judge), the devil tries to entice as many people as possible to his side. It is a battle he wages with the desperation of one who knows he is already defeated, knowing "that his time is short" (Rev 12:12). Therefore, Paul tells us in all honesty that "we are not contending against flesh and blood, but against the principalities, against the powers, against the world rulers of this present darkness, against the spiritual hosts of wickedness in the heavenly places" (Eph 6:12).

Scripture tells us that angels and demons (I want particularly to mention Satan) are spiritual creatures but also that they are individuals gifted with intelligence, will, freedom, and initiative. Those modern theologians who identify Satan with the abstract idea of evil are completely mistaken. Theirs is true heresy; that is, it is openly in contrast with the Bible, the Fathers, and the Magisterium of the Church. The truth about Satan was never doubted in the past; therefore, there are no dogmatic definitions in this respect with the exception of the following statement of the Fourth Lateran Council: "The devil [that is, Satan] and the other demons were created good by God; but they became evil through their own fault." Whoever denies Satan also denies sin and no longer understands the actions of Christ.

Let us be clear about this: Jesus defeated Satan through his sacrifice. However, Jesus also defeated Satan before his death, through his teachings: "If it is by the finger of God that I cast out demons, then the kingdom of God has come upon you" (Lk 11:20). Jesus is the strongest one, who tied up Satan (Mk 3:27), despoiled him, and pillaged his kingdom, which is at an end (Mk 3:26). Jesus first gave the power to cast out demons to his apostles; then he extended the power to the seventy-two disciples, and in the end he granted it to all those who would believe in him.

The Acts of the Apostles tell us that after the descent of the Holy Spirit the apostles continued to expel demons, and all Christians have done so after them. Already, the earliest Fathers of the Church, such as Justin and Irenaeus, clearly express Christian thought about the devil and about the power to cast him out. Other Fathers, in particular Tertullian and Origen, concur. These four authors alone can refute many modern theologians, who, for all purposes, either do not believe in the devil or completely ignore him.

The Second Vatican Council powerfully reminded us of this abiding teaching of the Church: "For a monumental struggle against the powers of darkness pervades the whole history of man. The battle was joined from the very origins of the world" (*Gaudium et Spes*, no. 37). "Although he was made by God in a state of holiness, from the very dawn of history man abused his liberty, at the urging of personified Evil. Man set himself against God and sought to find fulfillment apart from God. Although he knew God, he did not glorify Him as God, but his senseless mind was darkened and he served the creature rather than the Creator" (no. 13). "For He sent His Son, clothed in our flesh, in order that through this Son He might snatch men from the power of darkness and of Satan" (*Ad Gentes*, no. 3). How can those who deny the existence and the many activities of Satan understand the achievements of Christ? How can they understand the value of the redemptive death of Christ? On the basis of Sacred Scripture, the Second Vatican Council affirms that "[Christ], by His death and resurrection, had freed us from the power of Satan" (*Sacrosanctum Concilium*, no. 6). And "[Christ] was crucified and rose again to break the stranglehold of personified Evil" (*Gaudium et Spes*, no. 2).

Satan, defeated by Christ, fights against his followers. The battle against the evil spirits "was joined from the very origins of the world, and will continue until the last day, as the Lord has attested" (no. 37). During this time, every man is on battle alert because life on earth is a trial of faithfulness to God. "We strive therefore to please the Lord in all things (cf. 2 Cor 5:9). We put on the armor of God that we may be able to stand against the wiles of the devil and resist on the evil day. . . . For before we reign with the glorious Christ, all of us will be made manifest 'before the tribunal of Christ, so that each one may receive what he has won through the body, according to his works, whether good or evil' (2 Cor 5:10)" (*Lumen Gentium*, no. 48).

Even if this battle against Satan concerns all men and all times, there is no doubt that Satan's power is felt more keenly in periods of history when the sinfulness of the community is more evident. For example, when I view the decadence of the Roman Empire, I can see the moral disintegration of that period in history. Now we are at the same level of decadence, partly as a result of the misuse of the mass media (which are not evil in themselves) and partly because of Western consumerism and materialism, which have poisoned our society.

I believe that Pope Leo XIII, in a vision that will be detailed in the appendix of this chapter (pp. 37–39) received a prophetic warning concerning this demonic attack on our times. How does the devil oppose God and our Savior? By claiming for himself the adoration due to God and by mimicking Christian institutions. Therefore, he is anti-Christ and anti-Church. Satan uses the idolatry of sex, which reduces the human body to an instrument of sin, against the Incarnation of the Word who redeemed man by becoming man. Satan uses his churches, his cult, his devotees (often consecrated through a pact of blood), his adorers, the followers of his promises, to mimic the worship due to God. Just as Christ gave his apostles and their followers specific powers for the good of body and soul, so Satan gives specific powers to his followers for the destruction of body and soul. We will examine these specific powers in our explanation of witchcraft.

I will mention one more item on this subject. Just as it would be wrong to deny the existence of Satan, it is also wrong to accept the prevalent opinion that there are spiritual beings that are not mentioned in the Bible. These are the invention of spiritists, of followers of the occult, of those who espouse reincarnation, or of those who believe in "wandering souls". There are no good spirits other than angels; there are no evil spirits other than demons. Two Councils of the Church (Lyons and Florence) tell us that the souls of those who die go immediately to heaven or to hell or to purgatory. The souls of the dead who are present during seances or the souls of the dead who are present in living bodies to torture them are none other than demons. God allows a soul to return to earth only in very rare, exceptional cases, but we recognize that this subject is still full of unknowns. Father La Grua attempts to explain some of his own experiences with souls who are possessed by the devil, but I must reiterate that this is a matter that requires further research, and I will address it in a different book.

Some people marvel at the ability of demons to tempt man and even to own the body (but they can never take the soul unless man freely gives it to them) through possession and oppression. We should remember what is written in Revelation (12:7, etc.): "Now war arose in heaven, Michael and his angels fighting against the dragon; and the dragon and his angels fought, but they were defeated and there was no longer any place for them in heaven. And the great dragon was thrown down, that ancient serpent, who is called the Devil and Satan, the deceiver of the whole world—he was thrown down to the earth, and his angels were thrown down with him. . . . And when the dragon saw that he had been thrown down to the earth, he pursued the woman", who was "dressed like the sun", from whom Jesus was born (it is very clear that we are also talking about the Most Holy Virgin Mary). When the dragon realized that his efforts had failed, "he went off to make war on the rest of her offspring, on those who keep the commandments of God and bear testimony to Jesus."

During a May 24, 1987, visit to the Sanctuary of Saint Michael the Archangel, John Paul II said, "The battle against the devil, which is the principal task of Saint Michael the archangel, is still being fought today, because the devil is still alive and active in the world. The evil that surrounds us today, the disorders that plague our society, man's inconsistency and brokenness, are not only the results of original sin, but also the result of Satan's pervasive and dark action."

The last sentence is a clear reference to God's condemnation of the serpent, in Genesis (3:15): "I will put enmity between you and the woman, and between your seed and her seed; he shall bruise your head, and you shall bruise his heel." Is Satan already in hell? When did the battle between angels and devils take place? We cannot answer these questions unless we keep in mind that hell is more a state of mind than a place. Place and time are different concepts for spirits.

Revelation tells us that demons were hurled down to earth; therefore their final damnation has yet to happen, even if it is irrevocable. This means that they still have the power that God had given them, even if only "for a brief time". That is why they ask Jesus, "Have you come here to torment us before the time?" (Mt 8:29). Christ is the only judge; he will gather to himself his Mystical Body. This, then, is how we should interpret Paul's statement to the Corinthians, "since we are to judge angels" (1 Cor 6:3). When the "legion" of demons who possessed the man from Gerasa pleaded with Christ "not to command them to depart into the abyss" (Lk 8:31–32), they were seeking to hold on to their power. To a demon, leaving the body of a person and sinking into hell is an irrevocable death sentence; that is why the demon fights it to the last. However, his eternal pain will increase proportionately to the suffering he caused on earth. It is Saint Peter who tells us that the demons have not yet been definitively sentenced: "When angels sinned, God did not spare them; he sent them down to the underworld and consigned them to the dark underground caves to be held there till the day of judgment" (2 Pet 2:4). The glory of the angels, too, will be increased according to their good deeds; therefore, it is very useful to invoke their help.

What harm can the devil cause to the living? There are few books on the subject and a lack of common language. I will now attempt to define the words that I will use in this book.

Ordinary activity. This is "temptation", which is the most common activity of the demons, and it is directed against all men. When Jesus allowed Satan to tempt him, he accepted our human condition. I will not talk about this common diabolical endeavor, because the purpose of this book is to highlight Satan's *"extraordinary activity"*, which can take place only if God so allows.

This second category can take six different forms:

1. *External physical pain caused by Satan.* We know of this from many lives of the saints. We know that Saint Paul of the Cross, the Curé of Ars, Padre Pio, and many others were beaten, flogged, and pummeled by demons. This external form of persecution does not affect the soul; therefore with this type there has never been the need for an exorcism, only for prayers. Here I will dwell only on the other types of actions that directly affect exorcists.

2. *Demonic possession.* This occurs when Satan takes full possession of the body (not the soul); he speaks and acts without the knowledge or consent of the victim, who therefore is morally blameless. It is the gravest and most spectacular form of demonic afflictions, and it attracts the attention of producers of movies such as *The Exorcist.* According to the *Ritual* for exorcisms, some of the signs of possession include: speaking in tongues, extraordinary strength, and revealing the unknown. The man of Gerasa is a clear Gospel example of possession. To fix a set "model" for demonic possession would be a serious mistake; the affliction runs the gamut of symptoms and severity. For instance, I have exorcised two totally possessed persons who remained perfectly still and silent during the exorcism. I could cite many other examples and as many different symptoms.

3. *Diabolical oppression.* Symptoms vary from a very serious to a mild illness. There is no possession, loss of consciousness, or involuntary action and word. The Bible gives us many examples of oppression; one of them is Job. He was not possessed, but he lost his children, his goods, and his health. The bent woman and the deaf and dumb man who were cured by Jesus were not subject to total possession, but there was a demonic presence that caused physical

discomfort. Saint Paul was most certainly not possessed by a demon, but he had a demonic oppression that caused an evil affliction: "And to keep me from being too elated by the abundance of revelations, a thorn was given me in the flesh, a messenger of Satan, to harass me" (2 Cor 12:7). There is no doubting the evil origin of the affliction.

While possessions are still relatively rare today, we exorcists run into a great number of people who have been struck by the devil in their health, jobs, or relationships. We must make it clear that to diagnose and heal an oppression-related illness is not any easier than to diagnose and cure a person afflicted by full possession. The degree of gravity may be different, but the difficulty of the diagnosis and the amount of time involved in healing are the same.

4. *Diabolic obsession*. Symptoms include sudden attacks, at times ongoing, of obsessive thoughts, sometimes even rationally absurd, but of such nature that the victim is unable to free himself. Therefore the obsessed person lives in a perpetual state of prostration, desperation, and attempts at suicide. Almost always obsession influences dreams. Some people will say that this is evidence of mental illness, requiring the services of a psychiatrist or a psychologist. The same could be said of all other forms of demonic phenomena. Some symptoms, however, are so inconsistent with known illnesses that they point with certainty to their evil origins. Only an expert and well-trained eye can identify the crucial differences.

5. *Diabolic infestation*. Infestations affect houses, things, or animals. This book will only mention the topic. I merely want to state that I will never use this term when I refer to persons. I will always talk about possession, oppression, and obsession.

6. *Diabolical subjugation, or dependence*. People fall into this form of evil when they voluntarily submit to Satan. The two most common forms of dependence are the blood pact with the devil and the consecration to Satan.

How can we defend ourselves from all these evils? A strict interpretation of the *Ritual* confines the use of exorcisms only to instances of true possession. However, as I stated before, the current *Ritual* fails to address many occasions in which an exorcist diagnoses an evil influence. In all cases when there is no possession, the usual means to obtain grace should be sufficient. These means are prayer; the sacraments; almsgiving; leading a Christian life; pardoning offenses; and soliciting the aid of our Lord, Mary, the saints, and the angels. I will now say a few words about the angels. I gladly end this chapter on the devil, Christ's adversary, by speaking about the angels. They are our great allies. We owe them a great debt, and it is a mistake to mention them as rarely as we do. Every one of us has a guardian angel, most faithful of friends twenty-four hours a day, from conception to death. He unceasingly protects us, body and soul, while we, for the most part, never think about him. We also know that each nation has its particular guardian angel and, probably, every community and family, although we are not certain on the two last points. We know, however, that the angels are a multitude, and their desire to help us is much greater than Satan's desire to destroy us.

Sacred Scripture often tells us about the missions that God entrusted to his angels. We know the name of the prince of the angels, Saint Michael. There is a hierarchy among the angels based on love, which is guided by the divine intellect "in whose Will we find our peace", as Dante says. We also know the names of two other archangels:

Gabriel and Raphael. The Apocrypha add a fourth name, Uriel. Sacred Scripture divides the angels into nine choirs: dominions, powers, thrones, principalities, virtues, angels, archangels, cherubim, and seraphim. The believer who lives in the presence of the Trinity and is certain of its life within himself knows that he also has a mother, God's own Mother, who ceaselessly helps him. He knows that he can always count on the help of the angels and of the saints; therefore, how can he feel alone, abandoned, or oppressed by evil? In the life of the believer there is pain, because it is the way of the Cross that saves us, but there is no room for sadness. He who believes is always ready to give witness, to those who ask him, about the hope that sustains him (see 1 Pet 3:15).

It is also clear that the believer must be faithful to God and must fear sin. This is the basis of our strength, as Saint John tells us: "We know that any one born of God does not sin, but He who was born of God keeps him, and the evil one does not touch him" (1 Jn 5:18). If sometimes our weakness leads us to fall, we must immediately pick ourselves up with that great gift of God's mercy: repentance and confession.

Appendices

The Diabolical Vision of Pope Leo XIII

Many people will remember that, before the reforms of the Second Vatican Council, at the end of every Mass the celebrant and the faithful knelt to recite a prayer to Mary and one to Michael the Archangel. This is a very beautiful prayer and brings great benefits to all those who pray it.

> Saint Michael the Archangel, defend us in battle, be our protector against the wickedness and snares of the devil; may God rebuke him, we humbly pray; and do thou, O Prince of the heavenly host, by the power of God, thrust into hell Satan and all the evil spirits who wander through the world for the ruin of souls. Amen.

What are the origins of this prayer? Here is what the magazine *Ephemerides Liturgicae* reported in 1995 on pages 58–59:

> Father Domenico Pechenino writes: "I do not remember the exact year. One morning the great Pope Leo XIII had celebrated a Mass and, as usual, was attending a Mass of thanksgiving. Suddenly, we saw him raise his head and stare at something above the celebrant's head. He was staring motionlessly, without batting an eye. His expression was one of horror and awe; the color and look on his face changing rapidly. Something unusual and grave was happening in him.
>
> "Finally, as though coming to his senses, he lightly but firmly tapped his hand and rose to his feet. He headed for his private office. His retinue followed anxiously and solicitously, whispering: 'Holy Father, are you not feeling well? Do you need anything?' He answered: 'Nothing, nothing.' About half an hour later, he called for the Secretary of the

Congregation of Rites and, handing him a sheet of paper, requested that it be printed and sent to all the ordinaries around the world. What was that paper? It was the prayer that we recite with the people at the end of every Mass. It is the plea to Mary and the passionate request to the Prince of the heavenly host, beseeching God to send Satan back to hell."

Pope Leo XIII instructed to kneel during those prayers. What we just reported was published in the newspaper *La settimana del clero,* March 30, 1947, but it does not give the source of the information. However, we were able to verify that the prayer was indeed sent to the ordinaries in 1886, under unusual circumstances. A reliable witness, Cardinal Nasalli Rocca, in his 1946 Lenten Pastoral Letter to the Diocese of Bologna, wrote: "Leo XIII himself wrote that prayer. The sentence 'The evil spirits who wander through the world for the ruin of souls' has a historical explanation that was many times repeated by his private secretary, Monsignor Rinaldo Angeli. Leo XIII truly saw, in a vision, demonic spirits who were congregating on the Eternal City (Rome). The prayer that he asked all the Church to recite was the fruit of that experience. He would recite that prayer with strong, powerful voice: we heard it many a time in the Vatican Basilica. Leo XIII also personally wrote an exorcism that is included in the Roman *Ritual* (1954 edition, XII, C. III, p. 863 and following). He recommended that bishops and priests read these exorcisms often in their dioceses and parishes. He himself would recite them often throughout the day."

Another interesting factor attests to the value of the prayers that we used to recite after every Mass. Pius XI added a particular intention for the conversion of Russia (allocution of June 30, 1930). In this allocution, after reminding all to pray for Russia, and of the religious persecution in Russia, he closed with the following sentence: "Let us proclaim the prayers that our great predecessor, Leo XIII, directed all priests and the faithful to pray at the end of the Mass, for the particular intention of the conversion of Russia. Let all bishops and clergy so inform everyone who is present at the Holy Sacrifice, and remind them often" (*Civiltà cattolica*, 1930, vol. 3).

As we can see, the popes remind us often of the terrible presence of Satan among us. Additionally, the recommendation of Pope Pius XI strikes at the core of the false doctrines that are so prevalent in our century and that continue to poison the lives not only of theologians but of all people. The fact that the directives of Pius XI were not followed is the fault of those whose task it was to implement them. These directives were given before the Fatima apparitions became known throughout the world, and they were independent from—but were well in keeping with—the charismatic events with which the Lord blessed humanity through these apparitions.

The Gifts of Satan

Satan has the authority to give certain powers to his faithful. Since the devil is truly a liar, at times those who receive these powers either are not or do not want to be aware of their origin; they are all too happy to receive these free gifts. It may happen that one person is given the gift of clairvoyance. Others, simply by sitting in front of a blank piece of paper with a pen in their hands, are able to write page after page of spontaneous messages. Yet others feel that they can bilocate and that part of them can enter buildings even far away. It is very common for many to hear "a voice" that at times suggests prayers and at other times anything but prayers.

I could go on with the list. What is the source of these particular gifts? Are these charisms from the Holy Spirit? Is their origin satanic? Are these simply metaphysical gifts? To be able to discern the truth, we must turn to those who have experience in this matter. When Paul was at Thyatira, he was constantly followed by a slave woman who had the gift of clairvoyance and thereby earned much money for her masters. This was a gift that originated with Satan, and it disappeared immediately after Saint Paul expelled the evil spirit (Acts 16:16–18).

I will give the example of a witness who calls himself "Erasmus of Bari", as published in the magazine *Rinnovamento dello Spirito Santo* in September 1987. The parenthetical notes are my own.

> A few years ago, I experienced the game of *the glass*, without realizing that it was a form of spiritism. The messages that I received during this game spoke of *peace* and brotherhood (notice how the devil can conceal himself under the appearance of good deeds). Sometime later, while I was in Lourdes practicing my ministry, I was given strange faculties (this is also noteworthy; there are no places, no matter how sacred, where the devil cannot enter).
>
> Parapsychology defines the faculties that I was given as extrasensorial, that is, clairvoyance, mind reading, medical diagnosing, reading of hearts and lives of people both living and dead, and other powers. A few months later I received another faculty: the ability to take away pain merely by the imposition of hands. I could eliminate or alleviate any sort of suffering; could this be "prana therapy"?
>
> With all these powers, I had no difficulty contacting people, but after our meetings, they would walk away, shocked at my conversation and profoundly disturbed because I could see in their soul, and condemned the sins that they committed. However, as I was reading God's word, I realized that nothing had changed in my life. I continued to be quick to anger, slow in pardoning, easily resentful, and given to take offense at nothing. I was afraid to pick up my cross, I was afraid of the future and of death.

After a long journey in search of answers and many painful experiences, Jesus directed me to the renewal movement. There, I found brothers who prayed over me, and we realized that what happened to me was of diabolical origin, and not divine. I can witness that I have seen the power of the Name of Jesus. I recognized and confessed my past sins, I rejected every form of the occult. These powers came to an end and God forgave me; for this, I thank him.

Let us not forget that the Bible gives us examples of extraordinary deeds performed by God and by the devil. Some of the wonders that Moses performed at God's command before Pharaoh were mimicked by the court's magicians. That is why wonders of this kind, taken by themselves, do not point to their source.

Often those who are struck by evil disturbances are gifted with particular "sensitivities". For instance, they are able immediately to sense negativity in others, they can foresee future events, or at times they have a strong tendency to "lay hands" on psychologically fragile people. Other times they feel that they can influence others' lives, wishing them ill with a meanness, almost a dominance, that comes from within. I have witnessed that there is only one way to be healed of these disturbances; that is to fight and conquer these tendencies.

EXORCISMS

"These signs will accompany those who believe: in my name they will cast out demons" (Mk 16:17). This power, which Jesus granted to all those who believed in him, is still fully effective. It is a general power, based on prayer and faith. It can be exercised by individuals and by communities. It is always available and does not require special authorization. However, we must make it clear that in this case we are talking about *prayers of deliverance*, not of exorcisms.

To increase the effectiveness of this Christ-given power and to guard the faithful from magicians and charlatans, the Church instituted a specific sacramental, exorcism. It can be administered exclusively by bishops and by those priests (therefore, *never by lay persons*) who have received specific and direct license to exorcise. Canon Law (canon 1172), which governs exorcisms, reminds us that sacramentals, in contrast to private prayer (canon 1166), are also endowed with the Church's power of petition. Canon 1167 explains how sacramentals must be administered and which rites and Church-approved formulas are to be used.

When we take all this into consideration, we draw the obvious conclusion that only an authorized priest, besides the exorcist-bishop himself (I wish there were some!), can claim the title of exorcist. Today this title is abused. Many, both priests and lay people, claim to be exorcists when they are not. And many claim to perform exorcisms, while—at best—they simply intone prayers of deliverance and—at worst—they practice witchcraft.

Only the sacramental instituted by the Church can be called "exorcism". Any other use of the name is misleading and deceptive. According to the *Catechism of the Catholic Church*, there are only two types of exorcism: the sacrament of baptism, which is the only form of "simple exorcism", and the sacramental reserved to exorcists, which is called "solemn exorcism" (CCC 1673). It is a mistake to call exorcisms those forms of private or common intercessory prayers that in reality are only prayers of deliverance.

The exorcist must follow the prayers in the *Ritual*. There is one primary difference between exorcism and all other sacramentals, which is that an exorcism can last a few minutes or many hours. Therefore, it may not be necessary to intone all the prayers in the *Ritual*, or it may be necessary to add many other prayers, as suggested by the same *Ritual*.

The purpose of exorcism is twofold; the one purpose that is mentioned in all books on the subject is the liberation of those who are obsessed. However, the starting point and the first purpose, that of diagnosis, is all too often ignored. It is true that, before beginning, the exorcist questions the individual himself or his relatives to ascertain if the exorcism is necessary. But it is also true that *only through the exorcism itself* can we determine with certainty whether there is a satanic influence. Every phenomenon that we encounter, no matter how strange or inexplicable, may have a natural explanation. Even when we are faced with a multitude of psychiatric and parapsychological phenomena, we may not have sufficient data for a diagnosis. It is only through an actual exorcism that we can be certain whether we are dealing with satanic influence or not.

At this point we must introduce a topic that unfortunately is not covered by the *Ritual* itself and that is unknown by all those who have written on the subject.

I have stated that an exorcism's first and foremost purpose is diagnostic. That is, we must ascertain whether the symptoms are caused by an evil influence or by natural causes. In chronological sequence, this is the first objective that we seek and reach. However, in terms of importance, the specific end of exorcisms is the liberation from evil presence or ailment. It is extremely important to keep in mind this logical sequence of events (first the diagnosis and then the cure) that the exorcist must use to assess *the signs* correctly. It is also very important to recognize the signs that occur *before* an exorcism, *during* an exorcism, and *after* an exorcism and the development of signs *during the course of* the exorcism.

We believe that, indirectly, the *Ritual* addresses this succession of events, since it sets a norm (no. 3) warning the exorcist not to be too quick to detect a satanic presence. The *Ritual* then sets other norms warning the exorcist against the many tricks that Satan uses to disguise his presence. We exorcists believe that it is right to guard against being fooled by those who are psychologically ill, or not subject to any demonic influence, and therefore do not need us in any way. However, there is also the opposite danger—and today it is much more frequent and therefore more to be feared—the danger of not recognizing an evil presence and of denying an exorcism when it is requested. An unnecessary exorcism never harmed anyone; all the exorcists whom I questioned agree with me. The first time and in questionable situations, all of us use short, whispered exorcisms that can be mistaken for simple blessings; we have never regretted doing this. On the other hand, we have had reason to regret our inability to recognize the evil presence on those rare occasions when we denied an exorcism and a much more entrenched demonic activity was later detected.

The importance of recognizing the signs bears emphasizing; even few and uncertain signs are sufficient to proceed with the exorcism. If, during a session, we detect additional signs, we will continue for as long as necessary, even if the first exorcism is practiced relatively quickly. It is possible that, while we notice no signs during an exorcism, the patient later experiences considerable benefits from the session. At this point we repeat the exorcism; if the benefits continue, sooner or later the signs will be evident during the exorcism itself. I continue to stress that it is most useful to watch for the development of these signs as the exorcism progresses. When the signs begin to diminish gradually, it is usually an indication that healing has started. When the signs increase and follow an unpredictable pattern, it usually announces the surfacing of a previously hidden evil presence. Only when everything has surfaced can the healing begin.

From what we have said so far, we can understand how silly it is to wait to perform an exorcism until we are certain of satanic possession. It is also the result of complete inexperience to expect, before exorcisms, certain types of signs that are usually present only during, after, or as a result of many exorcisms. I have encountered some cases that required years of exorcisms before the sickness manifested all its seriousness. It is useless to try to reduce to standard models the behavior of those under evil influence. The more experienced exorcists are better able to recognize with certainty most forms of demonic manifestations. For example, the three signs that the *Ritual* cites as symptoms of satanic possession are talking in unknown languages, exhibiting superhuman strength, and knowing what is hidden; it is my significant experience, and that of all the other exorcists whom I questioned, that these signs always surfaced *during* an exorcism, never before. It would be unrealistic to expect the manifestation of those signs before proceeding with the exorcism.

However, we cannot always arrive at a precise diagnosis. Often we are faced with situations that leave us perplexed. This is because often, in the most difficult cases, we are faced with individuals who are afflicted both by evil influences and psychological disturbances. In these cases, a psychiatrist is a valuable help. Father Candido many times called on Professor Mariani, head of a famous Roman hospital for the mentally ill, to help him during an exorcism. And many times Professor Mariani invited Father Candido to help him diagnose and eventually cure some of his patients.

I have to laugh when some modern "experts" in theology state, as though it were a great novelty, that certain types of mental illnesses can be confused with diabolical possession. Some psychiatrists or parapsychologists make the same statements, thinking that they have invented the wheel! If they were more knowledgeable, they would know that the first experts to caution about making this diagnostic mistake have been the ecclesiastic authorities themselves. Since 1583, when it appeared among the decrees of the synod of Reims, the Church gave warning about the danger of mistaking mental illness for diabolical possession. But in those days, the science of psychiatry had not been born yet, and theologians believed in the Gospel.

Exorcisms, in addition to diagnosing, aim at healing the patient by freeing him from demonic influences; a long and often difficult journey starts here. The cooperation of the possessed individual, which is necessary to make progress, is often hindered: he should pray, and often he cannot. He should receive the sacraments frequently, and he is not able to. At times, even going to the exorcist to receive the sacramentals seems like an insurmountable task. He needs help from others, but in the majority of cases, nobody understands him.

How long does it take to free someone from demons? This is a question that has no answer. He who frees is the Lord; he acts with divine freedom, even though he most surely listens to prayers, especially if offered through the intercession of the Church. Generally, we can say that the time factor is proportionate to the initial strength of the diabolical possession and the length of time before seeking exorcism. I recall a girl of fourteen, who had been possessed only a few days. She seemed to be furious; she kicked, bit, and scratched. It required only fifteen minutes of exorcism to free her completely. At one point, she dropped to the ground as though dead—almost like the Gospel narration of the young man whom the apostles were unable to heal. After a few minutes she recovered her senses and started running around in the courtyard with one of her younger brothers.

The instances of such a rapid healing, however, are extremely rare or happen when the evil influence is minimal. Most of the time the exorcist deals with severe cases, because nobody thinks of the exorcist anymore. I will give a typical example. A child exhibits strange behavior. The parents do not seek the causes; they think that the child will outgrow it, especially since, at the beginning, the symptoms are light. When the phenomena become worse, the parents begin to seek medical help; they try first one doctor, then another, with no results. Once a seventeen-year-old girl came to me. After visiting the most reputable hospitals in Europe, some friends or a misguided acquaintance suggested the possibility of some unnatural influence and recommended the services of a witch doctor. At this point, the initial damage was multiplied. By pure chance, following who knows whose advice (almost never that of priests) she turned to me for help. This process took place over a period of many years, and the evil influence had taken deep root. The first exorcism speaks of "uprooting and putting to flight" the devil, and rightly so. Situations like this one require many sessions, often lasting many years, and deliverance is not always possible.

I repeat: the time element belongs to God. The faith of the exorcist and the faith of the one being exorcised are very helpful, just as are the prayers of the victim, his family, and other faithful (such as cloistered nuns, parish communities, prayer groups, and particularly those groups that focus on deliverance prayers). The appropriate sacramentals, such as exorcised water, or at least holy water, exorcised oil, and exorcised salt, when used in conjunction with the goals indicated by the prayers of deliverance, are extremely beneficial. Any priest can exorcise water, oil, and salt, and an exorcist is not required. However, it is necessary that the priest believe in and be familiar with these specific blessings in the *Ritual*. Priests who are aware of these sacramentals are very rare; the majority do not know of their existence and laugh at anyone who requests them. I will return to the subject later in the book.

Frequent reception of the sacraments and a life lived according to the teachings of the Gospel are of fundamental importance. The power of the Rosary and devotion to the Virgin Mary are well documented. Less powerful is the intercession of angels and saints. Pilgrimages to sanctuaries are extremely fruitful. Sanctuaries often are built on sites specifically chosen by God as places where a deliverance from evil that began with exorcisms can be completed.

God has showered us with numerous means of grace; it is up to us to make good use of them. When the Gospel narrates the story of the temptations of Christ at the hands of Satan, it significantly tells us that Jesus uses sentences taken from the Bible to rebuke the tempter. The word of God is highly effective; prayers of praise—both spontaneous and especially biblical, such as the Psalms and hymns of praise to God—are most beneficial.

Even with all these graces, the efficacy of exorcisms forces much humility on the exorcist, precisely because he is able to experience firsthand that he is nothing, and he who acts is God. Both the exorcist and the person being exorcised undergo periods of severe discouragement; tangible fruits are often slow and hard to come by. On the other hand, the exorcist can also experience firsthand great spiritual fruits. These fruits help us in part to understand why the Lord allows these extremely painful trials. We go forward in the darkness with faith, with the awareness of walking toward the light.

I would like to add some reflections on the protective importance of sacred images, both on our bodies and on places such as the door of the house, in bedrooms, dining room, or the room most used by the family. The sacred image does not mimic the pagan custom of a "good-luck charm" but follows the Christian concept of imitating and seeking the protection of those who are represented by those images. Today I often walk into houses where a bright red horn is displayed on the front door, and when I go from room to room to bless them, I see very few sacred objects. It is a great mistake.

I remember the example of Bernardino of Siena, who would convince families to put on the front door of their houses a large medal with the initials of the name of Jesus

(JHS, that is, *Jesus Hominum Salvator*—Jesus, Savior of Men) as a memento of his very popular missions.

I personally experienced many times the efficacy of medals worn with faith. The miracles attributed to the Miraculous Medal alone, a medal that has been distributed by the millions all over the world, after the apparitions of the Virgin to Saint Catherine Labouré (Paris, 1830), are so many that it would be impossible to list them all. There are many books that deal directly with this subject.

One of the most famous instances of diabolical possession, which many books report, thanks to the accuracy of the historical documentation, concerns two brothers, the Burners, in Illfur, Alsatia. The two brothers were freed in 1869, following a series of exorcisms. It is reported that among the many, extremely vicious, actions of the demon was a plan to overturn the coach that transported the exorcist, a monsignor, and a nun. The devil was foiled in his intent only because the coach driver, at the last minute, was given a medal of Saint Benedict to protect him on the journey, and the good man devoutly put it in his pocket.

Finally, I call to mind the four paragraphs of the *Catechism of the Catholic Church* dedicated to exorcisms. If we read them in a sequence that we find to be a logical progression, these are:

Paragraph 517 talks about Christ the Redeemer and his healings and exorcisms. This is the starting point of Christ's actions.

Paragraph 550 states that "the coming of God's kingdom means the defeat of Satan's"; these words of Jesus are quoted: "If it is by the Spirit of God that I cast out demons, then the kingdom of God has come upon you" (Mt 12:28). This is the final goal of exorcisms: with the deliverance of those possessed by the devil we demonstrate the complete victory of Christ over the prince of the world.

The following two paragraphs tell of the twofold progression followed by exorcisms: one as a component of baptism, and the other as power of freedom for those who are obsessed.

Paragraph 1237 reminds us that baptism is liberation from sin and from the slavery to Satan. Therefore, one or more exorcisms are pronounced over the candidate, who explicitly renounces Satan.

Paragraph 1673 affirms that the Church, through the exorcism, authoritatively and publicly asks, in the name of Jesus Christ, that a person or object be protected against the influence of the evil one and withdrawn from his dominion. The exorcism aims to cast out demons or to liberate from demonic influences.

I stress the importance of this last paragraph, which fills two gaps in the current *Ritual* and in the *Code of Canon Law*. In fact, it speaks of liberating not only people but also objects (this is a generic term that can include houses, animals, and things, according to tradition). Canon Law makes exorcisms applicable to demonic influences and not only demonic possession.

TARGETS OF THE EVIL ONE

I am often asked whether many are struck by the evil one. I can answer with the opinion expressed by a famous French exorcist, the Jesuit Father Tonquedec: "There are a vast number of unhappy souls who, while not showing signs of demonic possession, turn to the exorcist to be relieved of their sufferings, such as stubborn illnesses, adversities, all sorts of misfortunes. Those possessed by the devil are few, but these unhappy souls are legion."

This observation is still valid when we consider the vast difference between those who are truly struck and those who simply want the authoritative opinion of the exorcist concerning a succession of woes. Today, however, we must take into account many factors that were not present in Father Tonquedec's time. I have directly experienced these factors, and based on this experience I can state that the number of those who are affected by the evil one has greatly increased.

The first factor that influences the increase of evil influences is Western consumerism. The majority of people have lost their faith due to a materialistic and hedonistic lifestyle. I believe that a good portion of the blame is to be attributed to socialism and communism, especially in Italy, where Marxist doctrine has dominated the media and the culture in the past few years. It is estimated that barely 12 percent of the population of Rome attends Sunday Mass; it is a well-known fact that where religion regresses, superstition progresses. We can see the proliferation, especially among the young, of spiritism, witchcraft, and the occult. We can add to this the pursuit of yoga, Zen, transcendental meditation: these are all practices based on reincarnation, on dissolving the human person into divinity, or, in any case, on other doctrines that are unacceptable to Christians. We do not need to go to India anymore to find gurus; we can find them at our doorsteps. Often these apparently innocent practices bring about hallucinations and schizophrenic conditions. To this I can add the exponential proliferation of many sects, many of which bear a distinctly satanic mark.

Witchcraft and spiritism are taught on TV. Books on the occult are sold at newspaper stands and even through the mail. Then we can add the various collections of newspapers and horror shows where a satanic twist is added to sex and violence. And we cannot omit mentioning the growing popularity of a type of music that is almost obsessive; I refer in particular to satanic rock. Piero Mantero expands on this subject in his book *Satana e lo stratagemma della coda* (Udine: Segno, 1988). When I was invited to speak at a few high schools, I was able personally to verify how great is the influence of these tools of Satan on the young. It is unbelievable how widespread are witchcraft and spiritism, in all their forms, in middle and high school. This evil is everywhere, even in small towns.

I must point out that too many churchmen are totally disinterested in these problems, and so they leave the faithful defenseless. I believe that taking most of the exorcisms out of the baptismal ritual was a grave mistake (and it seems that Paul VI shared my opinion). I believe that it was a mistake to have eliminated, without a suitable replacement, the prayer to Saint Michael the Archangel that we used to recite after every Mass. I am convinced that allowing the ministry of exorcism to die is an unforgivable deficiency to be laid squarely at the door of bishops. Every diocese should have at least one exorcist at the cathedral, and every large parish and sanctuary should have one as well. Today the exorcist is seen as a rarity, almost impossible to find. His activity, on the other hand, has an indispensable pastoral value, as valuable as that of the preacher, the confessor, and those who administer the other sacraments.

The Catholic hierarchy must say a forceful *mea culpa*. I am personally acquainted with many Italian bishops; I know of only a few who have ever practiced or who have assisted during an exorcism or who are adequately aware of this problem. I do not hesitate to repeat what I have written elsewhere: if a bishop, when faced with a valid request for an exorcism—I am not talking about the request of some demented person—does not address the problem, either personally or by delegating the task to a qualified priest, he is guilty of a most serious sin of omission. As a result of this negligence, we now have lost what once was *the school*; in the past, a practicing exorcist would instruct a novice. I will return to this topic.

It is thanks to the movies that we find a renewed interest in exorcisms. Vatican Radio, on February 2, 1975, interviewed William Friedkin, the director of the movie *The Exorcist*, and his "expert advisor", the theologian Father Thomas Bemingan, S.J. The director stated that he wanted to tell the facts of an episode, narrated in a book, that had actually happened in 1949. The movie did not draw any conclusions concerning diabolic possession. According to the director, this was a question for theologians. When the Jesuit priest was asked if *The Exorcist* was just one of many horror movies or something altogether different, he emphatically maintained that it was the latter. He cited the great impact the movie had made on audiences throughout the world as a demonstration that —save some special effects—the film had dealt very soberly with the problem of evil, reawakening an interest in exorcisms that had been all but forgotten.

How can we fall prey to extraordinary satanic activity? By this I mean other than the ordinary activity—temptation—which applies to everyone. We can do so through our own fault or by being completely unaware. We can group the reasons into four categories: (1) with God's permission, (2) as innocent victims of an evil spell, (3) due to a grave and hardened sinful condition, (4) through association with evil people or places.

1. *With God's permission*. I want to make absolutely clear that nothing happens without God's permission. It is also absolutely clear that God does not wish evil for anyone, but he allows it when it is our will (since he created us with completely free will), and he can use everything, even evil, for our own good. The characteristic of the first category of extraordinary demonic activity is complete absence of human guilt; it is entirely due to a diabolical intervention. God always allows normal satanic activity—temptation— and gives us all the graces necessary to resist, with the resulting good of strengthening our spiritual life. In the same manner, God at times also allows extraordinary satanic activity—possession, evil influences—to increase our humility, patience, and mortification.

We have already given a couple of examples of this category: an external action of the devil that causes physical pain (such as the beatings and floggings suffered by the Curé of Ars and Padre Pio) or when a so-called oppression is allowed, as we have mentioned concerning Job and Saint Paul.

The lives of many saints include examples of this affliction. Among modern saints, I can cite two who have been beatified by Pope John Paul II: Father Giovanni Calabria and Sister Mary of Jesus Crucified (who was the first Arab to be beatified). In both cases, and without any human fault, they were subjected to periods of true satanic possession. During those periods, the two saints did and said things totally incompatible with their holiness without the least fault, because it was the devil who acted through their bodies.

2. *When we are subjected to an evil spell.* This is another case in which the victim is completely blameless. Here, however, there is some human activity, but it is performed by those who cast the spell or those who hire a witch to cast it. I will devote an entire chapter to this topic. Here I will simply say that an evil spell *is causing the suffering of others through the intervention of the devil.* This intervention can take many different forms: binding, the evil eye, a curse. I will say right away that the most common method is sorcery. Sorcery is also the most frequent cause that we encounter in those who are struck by possession or other evil influences. I do not understand the reasons behind the refusal of some churchmen who claim not to believe in sorcery, just as I cannot understand how they can protect from sorcery those among their flock who are victims of this evil.

Some may be surprised that God allows this sort of evil to happen. God created us free, and he never rejects his creatures, not even the most perverted. At the end, he rewards everyone according to his just deserts, because everyone will be judged according to his actions. In the meantime, if we use well the freedom that he gave us, we will gain merit; or we can use it for evil purposes, and we will earn blame. We can either help others or hurt them through many forms of abuse. To give an example: I can pay a killer to murder someone; God is not obligated to stop him. Just as easily, I can pay a warlock or a witch doctor to cast an evil spell on someone. God, just as in the first case, is not obligated to intervene, although in many cases he does. For instance, those who live in a state of grace, those who pray most fervently, have a much better chance of obtaining divine intervention against the evil one than those who do not practice their faith or, worse, who live in a habitual state of mortal sin.

Here I must give a warning that I will expand in a later chapter: the field of sorcery and other evil actions is the domain of swindlers. Instances of true sorcery are a minute percentage among the wholesale deceit that prevails in this arena. Besides offering a variety of opportunities to swindlers, sorcery is also particularly suited to suggestions and whims of feeble minds. Therefore, it is important that the exorcist be on guard against deception, but it is also important that everyone with common sense be vigilant too.

3. *A grave and hardened state of sin*. Here we are addressing the cause that today, unfortunately, is on the increase, with a resulting increase in the numbers of people who are victims of the devil. At the root, *the true cause is always a lack of faith*. As lack of faith increases, so does superstition; it is almost a mathematical reality. I believe that the Gospel gives us a clear example of this in the character of Judas. He was a thief. Who knows how many times Jesus tried to correct him and call him to repentance, and the only result was rejection and a hardening in sin. Judas reaches the

climax when he asks the chief priests, "What are you prepared to give me, if I hand him over to you?" (Mt 26:15). In the narrative of the Last Supper, the Gospel tells us that terrible sentence about Judas: "Then after the morsel, Satan entered into him" (Jn 13:27). I have no doubt that here it means true diabolic possession.

In the current environment, where we are witnessing the collapse of the family, I have encountered many cases of possessed people who, in addition to other sins, were living in irregular marriages. I have dealt many times with women whose sins included the crime of abortion. I have been confronted with numerous people who, in addition to sexual aberrations, committed other violent actions. Many times I have been faced with homosexuals who were drug addicts and who had committed drug-related sins. It is almost redundant to say that, in all these stages, the way to healing can begin only with a sincere conversion.

4. *Association with evil people and places.* This category includes the practice or assisting in the practice of seances, witchcraft, satanic cults, or sects—which culminate in black masses—the occult . . . associating with warlocks, witch doctors, or certain types of card readers. These are all activities that make us vulnerable to evil spells. If we go so far as to desire a relationship with Satan, there is such a thing as consecration to Satan, the blood pact with Satan, attendance at satanic schools, and the election to the priesthood of Satan. Unfortunately, in the past fifteen years, we have witnessed an increase, almost an explosion, of these types of associations.

A very common example of associating with warlocks or witch doctors is this: Someone who is the victim of a stubborn illness cannot find any remedy. Someone else experiences all sorts of misfortune and believes that it is due to an evil influence. They appeal to a card reader or a warlock, who tells them, "You are subject to an evil spell." Up to now, there is very little damage done. However, unfortunately what follows is something like this: "For one thousand dollars—or more—I will cure you." These fees can be as high as $35,000. If the individual agrees, the card reader or warlock asks for some personal item: a photograph, a piece of underwear, a lock of hair, a few hairs, or a nail clipping. At this point, the evil act is accomplished. What does the warlock do with these items? He obviously uses them to practice black magic.

Unfortunately, many fall victim to these individuals because these sorcerers are often women who are always seen in church, or because the room of the warlock is blanketed with crucifixes, portraits of saints, the Blessed Virgin, and portraits of Padre Pio. The victims are also often told, "I practice only white magic; if you asked me for black magic I would refuse." In current terminology, white magic means to take away a spell; black magic means to cast a spell. In reality, as Father Candido never ceased to repeat, there are no such things as "white" and "black" magic; there is only black magic. Every form of magic is practiced with recourse to Satan. Therefore, the poor victim who went to the warlock with a minor evil influence (or probably without any such influence) goes home with a true, full-blown one. When this occurs, often we exorcists have to work much harder after the ill-fated action of the warlocks than we would have if the person had come to us with the original complaint.

Many times, today as in the past, diabolic possession can be confused with psychological illnesses. I greatly esteem those psychiatrists who are professionally competent and know the limitations of their science. They are honestly able to recognize when one of their patients exhibits symptoms that go beyond any known disease. For instance, Professor Simone Morabito, of Bergamo, stated that he had positive proof that many who were considered mentally ill were in reality afflicted with satanic possession, and he was able to cure them with the aid of exorcists (see *Gents*, no. 5 [1990], pp. 106–12). I know of other similar instances, and I would like to give one particular example.

On April 24, 1988, Pope John Paul II beatified the Spanish Carmelite Father Francisco Palau. Father Palau is very interesting for our purposes because he devoted the last years of his life to those who were possessed by demons. He bought a hospice, in which he cared for the mentally ill. He exorcised all of them: those who were possessed were healed; those who were simply mentally ill remained ill. He encountered many obstacles in his ministry, mainly from other clergy. Twice he traveled to Rome, in 1866 to talk about his problems with Pius IX, and in 1879 to ask the First Vatican Council to reestablish the office of exorcist as a permanent ministry of the Church. We know that the Council was interrupted; nevertheless, the necessity to reestablish this pastoral service remains urgent.

Admittedly, it is difficult to distinguish between someone who is possessed and someone with psychological problems. However, an expert exorcist will be able to detect the difference more easily than a psychiatrist because the exorcist will keep his mind open to all possibilities and will be able to identify the distinguishing elements. The psychiatrist, in the majority of cases, does not believe in demonic possession; therefore he does not even consider it in his diagnostic process. Years ago, Father Candido was exorcising a young man who was diagnosed with epilepsy by the psychiatrist who was advising him. This doctor accepted the invitation to watch his young patient during an exorcism. When Father Candido touched the head of the youth with his hand, he fell to the ground in convulsions. "You see, Father, that we are obviously dealing with epilepsy", the doctor quickly pointed out. Father Candido bent down and again put his hand on the youth's head. He jumped up and remained standing, motionless. "Is this what epileptics do?" asked Father Candido. "No, never", answered the psychiatrist, obviously taken aback by that behavior. Father Candido's exorcisms eventually completely cured that young man, while for years, doctors and prescriptions—not to mention the high fees—had only harmed him.

Here we touch a sensitive nerve: in difficult cases, the diagnosis requires cooperation between different fields of expertise, as we will demonstrate in our final analysis. Unfortunately, those who pay for the experts' errors are always those who are ill and who all too often end up ruined by medical mistakes.

I very much appreciate scientists who, even if they are unbelievers, recognize the limitations of their science. Professor Emilio Servadio, who is an internationally renowned psychiatrist, psychoanalyst, and parapsychologist, made the following interesting statements on Vatican Radio. On February 2, 1975, he said:

> Science must stop when confronted with what cannot be explained or verified by known methods. Some of the limits cannot be identified with precision because we are not dealing with physical phenomena. I believe that every scientist who is aware of his responsibilities knows that his tools go so far and no farther. When it comes to demonic possession I

can speak only for myself and not on behalf of science. I have seen some instances where the evil and the destruction caused by certain phenomena present characteristics that truly cannot be mistaken for those encountered by a scientist such as a parapsychologist or a psychiatrist—for instance, when we deal with poltergeists or similar activities. It would be like trying to compare a mischievous boy with a sadistic criminal. There is a difference that cannot be measured with tools but that can be felt. In these situations I believe that a man of science must admit the presence of powers that cannot be ruled by science and that science cannot be called to define.

Appendix

Afraid of the Devil? Saint Teresa of Jesus Responds

I provide a passage from the autobiography of Saint Teresa of Avila to counteract unjustified fear of the devil. It is an encouraging passage, unless we ourselves open the door to the devil. (From *The Book of Her Life*, chap. 25, nos. 19–22, in *The Collected Works of St. Teresa of Avila*, trans. Kieran Kavanaugh, O.C.D., and Otilio Rodriguez, O.C.D., vol. 1, 2d ed. [Washington, D.C.: ICS Publications, 1987].)

If this Lord is powerful, as I see that He is and I know that He is, and if the devils are His slaves (and there is no doubt about this because it's a matter of faith), what evil can they do to me since I am a servant of this Lord and King? Why shouldn't I have the fortitude to engage in combat with all of hell?

I took a cross in my hand, and it seemed to me truly that God gave me courage because in a short while I saw that I was another person and that I wouldn't fear bodily combat with them; for I thought that with that cross I would easily conquer all of them. So I said: "Come now all of you, for, being a servant of the Lord, I want to see what you can do to me."

There was no doubt, in my opinion, that they were afraid of me, for I remained so calm and so unafraid of them all. All the fears I usually felt left me—even to this day. For although I sometimes saw them, as I shall relate afterward, I no longer had hardly any fear of them; rather it seemed they were afraid of me. I was left with a mastery over them truly given by the Lord of all; I pay no more attention to them than to flies. I think they're such cowards that when they observe they are esteemed but little, their strength leaves them.

These enemies don't know how to attack head-on, save those whom they see surrender to them, or when God permits them to do so for the greater good of His servants whom they tempt and torment. May it please His Majesty that we fear Him whom we ought to fear and understand that more harm can come to us from one venial sin than from all hell together—for this is so.

How frightened these devils make us because we want to be frightened through other attachments to honors, property, and delights! It is then that they do us great harm, when they are joined with us who loving and desiring what we ought to abhor are in contradiction with ourselves. For we make them fight against us with our own very weapons, handing over to them what we need for our own defense. This is a great pity. But if we abhor all for God and we embrace the cross and try truly to serve God, the devil will flee these truths like the plague. He is a friend of lies, and is the lie itself. He will make no pact with anyone who walks in truth. When he sees the intellect darkened, he subtly helps to blind the eyes. For if he sees people already blind by the fact that they place their trust in vain things (and so vain that these worldly things become like children's games), he concludes that they are then children, treats them as such, and dares to fight with them not once but many times.

May it please the Lord that I not be one of these but that His Majesty favor me so that I may understand by repose what repose is, by honor what honor is, and by delight what delight is—not the reverse; and a fig for all the devils, because they shall fear me. I don't understand these fears, "The devil! The devil!", when we can say "God! God", and make the devil tremble. Yes, for we already know that he cannot stir if the Lord doesn't permit him to. What is this? Without doubt, I fear those who have such great fear of the devil more than I do the devil himself, for he can't do anything to me. Whereas these others, especially if they are confessors, cause severe disturbance; I have undergone some years of such great trial that I am amazed now at how I was able to suffer it. Blessed be the Lord who has so truly helped me!

THE POINT OF DEPARTURE

One day, a bishop called and asked me to exorcise a certain person. At first I answered that it was his duty to appoint an exorcist. He replied that he had been unable to find a priest who would accept the task. Unfortunately, this is a common occurrence. Often priests do not believe in exorcisms, but if the bishop offers them the office of exorcist, they feel as though one thousand demons are upon them and refuse. Many times I have written that Satan is much more enraged when we take souls away from him through confession than when we take away bodies through exorcism. In fact, we cause the devil even greater rage by preaching, because faith sprouts from the word of God. Therefore, a priest who has the courage to preach and hear confessions should not be afraid to exorcise.

Léon Bloy wrote heated words against priests who refuse to exorcise. Balducci quotes them in *Il diavolo* (Piemme, p. 233): "Priests almost never use their powers of exorcist because they lack faith and are effectively afraid to disgust the demons." This is also true; many are afraid of reprisal and forget that the devil already causes all the harm that the Lord allows him; we can negotiate no peace treaties with him! The author goes on: "If priests have lost their faith to the point of not believing in their power of exorcism and do not use it anymore, this is a horrible misfortune, a cruel duplicity that leads to the irrevocable abandonment to the worst of enemies of those unfortunate souls who fill the hospitals and who are deemed victims of hysteria." Strong words, but true. It is a direct betrayal of a command of Christ.

Returning to the telephone call of that bishop. I told him frankly that if he could not find a priest, he was obligated to perform the exorcism personally. I heard him answer with artless candor, "Me? I would not know where to start." To which I retorted with the words that Father Candido used with me when I began my apprenticeship: "Start by reading the instructions in the *Ritual* and recite the prescribed prayers over the person who requested them."

This is the point of departure. The *Ritual* for exorcisms starts by listing twenty-one norms that must be followed by the exorcist. It does not matter that these norms were written in 1614; these directives—which can be expanded—are full of wisdom and are still valid today. The *Ritual* begins by cautioning the exorcist against an easy belief in the presence of a demon and gives a series of practical rules both to help recognize the presence of true possession and to guide the demeanor of the exorcist.

The confusion of the bishop ("I would not know where to start") is justified. We cannot improvise an exorcism. To assign such a task to any priest is like demanding that someone perform surgery after reading a textbook on the subject. Many, too many, things are not written in a text but are learned only through practice. That is why I decided to publish the experience that I gained under the direction of Father Candido's great expertise, even though I realize that what I will say is insufficient. It is one thing to read about something; it is another thing actually to see it. Nevertheless, what I will say cannot be found in any other book.

In reality, the starting point is different. When someone comes, or is brought by family or friends, to be exorcised, one starts with an examination to determine whether or not there are reasonable grounds for proceeding with an exorcism. Diagnosis can be made only by such an examination. *Therefore, one begins by studying the symptoms that are presented by the person or his relatives, as well as their possible cause.*

One begins with the physical symptoms. The two areas most commonly affected by evil influences are the head and the stomach. In addition to headaches that are severe and unresponsive to prescriptions, symptoms include a sudden inability to learn. In particular, young people who never had trouble at school all of a sudden cannot study anymore, and their ability to concentrate disappears. The signs listed in the *Ritual* are limited to the most spectacular manifestations of possession, such as the ability to speak or understand unknown languages perfectly, to know the hidden and the remote or to demonstrate a superhuman physical strength. As I have already mentioned, I was able to detect these signs only during the blessings (this is how I always refer to exorcisms), never before. Often I am told of strange or violent behavior. A typical symptom of evil influence is an aversion to the sacred. It happens then that prayerful people suddenly stop praying. Others stop going to church and become full of rage; some suddenly blaspheme often and act violently against sacred images. Almost always we also encounter asocial behavior, such as anger against relatives or acquaintances, and many types of bizarre behavior.

Needless to say, with few rare exceptions, those who land at an exorcist's door have already tried every possible medical test and remedy. Therefore, it is easy for the exorcist to discover the medical diagnosis, what therapy was attempted, and with what results.

The other area that is commonly affected by evil influences is the neck of the stomach, immediately under the sternum. There we find acute and piercing pains for which no cure can be found. If the pain travels, now to the entire stomach, then to the kidneys, later to the ovaries, etc., defying the understanding and remedies of medicine, it is a common indication of evil influence.

We can state that *"one of the determining factors in the recognition of diabolic possession is the inefficacy of medicines"*, while blessings prove very efficacious. I exorcised Mark, a young man who was the victim of a severe possession. He had been confined for a long time and had been tormented by psychiatric remedies, especially electroshock, without the slightest reaction. When the doctor prescribed sleep therapy, for an entire week they gave him enough sleeping pills to sedate an elephant; he never fell asleep, either during the day or during the night. He wandered around the hospital in a stupor, with wide-open eyes. Finally he landed at my doorstep, with immediate positive results.

Superhuman strength can also be a sign of diabolic possession. A demented person in an insane asylum can be immobilized with a straitjacket. A person possessed by demons cannot be immobilized; he can even break iron chains, as the man from Gerasa did in the Gospel. Father Candido told me of a thin, apparently weak girl who had to be subdued by force by four strong men during exorcisms. She broke every bond, even some heavy leather straps with which they tried to tie her down. Once, when she was tied with strong ropes to an iron bed, she broke some of the iron rods and folded others at a right angle.

Many times the patient—and his relatives, if the entire family is struck—hears strange noises, footsteps in the hallway, doors opening and closing, objects that disappear and reappear in the most unlikely places, and banging against furniture and walls. When I conduct my investigation into the causes, I always ask when the occurrences started, if they can be tied to something concrete, if the patient participated in seances, if he approached card readers, and, in case of a positive answer, how things have progressed.

It is possible that, at the suggestion of some friends or acquaintances, the pillow or mattress of the afflicted person was opened, and there were found the most interesting objects, such as colored threads, tufts of hair, tresses, wooden or iron slivers, rosaries or ribbons tied with the tightest of knots, puppets, animal shapes, blood clots, or pebbles; these are a certain proof of sorcery.

If, after investigating these factors, I am convinced that there is the intervention of an evil force, I will proceed with an exorcism.

I will now mention some examples. I will change the names or anything else that could lead to the identification of individuals. Martha and her husband came to me for a blessing. They came from quite a distance and sacrificed to pay for the trip. For many years, Martha had been treated by neurologists, without any result. After a few questions, I realized that I could proceed with an exorcism, even though others had vainly attempted to exorcise her. At the beginning, she fell to the ground and appeared to have fainted. As I proceeded with the introductory prayers, she would complain, from time to time, "I want a true exorcism, not these things!" When I began with the first exorcism, which begins with the words "*Exorcizo te*", she was satisfied and calmed down; she obviously remembered these words from her previous experiences. Then she began to complain that her eyes hurt. These are actions and signs not in keeping with someone who is possessed. When she came back, she could not discern whether my exorcism had helped her or not. Before dismissing her, since I still had some doubts, I brought her to Father Candido. After he placed his hand on her head, he told me immediately that the devil had nothing to do with her case. It was a matter for psychiatry, not exorcism.

Pierluigi, fourteen years old, was big and heavy for his age. He was unable to study; he drove his teachers and schoolmates crazy. He did not get along with anybody, but he was not violent. One of his characteristics was this: when he would sit on the ground with crossed legs (he called it "being an Indian"), no amount of force could lift him off the ground; it was as though he had turned into lead. After some fruitless medical treatments, he was brought to Father Candido, who, after he had established true demonic possession, began to exorcise him. Another characteristic of Pierluigi's was this: although he was not contentious, people became nervous around him and began shouting; they lost control. One day he sat cross-legged on the third-floor landing in his apartment complex. The other tenants went up and down the stairs and would shake him to make him move, but he would not. At one point, all the tenants of the building gathered together on the staircase, on the other landings and were shouting and yelling against Pierluigi like people possessed. Someone called the police; the boy's parents called Father Candido, who arrived just before the police and was chatting with the boy to convince him to go into his apartment. The policemen—three strong young men—told him: "Move over, Reverend, this is our business." When they tried to move Pierluigi, they could not budge him half an inch. Much surprised and dripping with perspiration, they did not know what to do. Then Father Candido told them, "Ask everyone to go back to his apartment", and in a minute, there was complete silence. Then he added, "You go down one flight of stairs and watch." They obeyed him. At the end, he told Pierluigi, "You were good: you did not say one word, but kept everyone at bay. Now let's go back home with me." He took the boy by the hand, and he rose and followed him, all happy, where his parents were waiting for him. After many exorcisms, Pierluigi improved considerably but was not completely liberated.

One of the most difficult instances that I remember involves a man—at one time very notorious—who went to Father Candido for many years to receive blessings. I also went to his house, where he was confined, to bless him. I performed the exorcism; he said nothing (he was possessed by a mute demon), and I could not see the slightest reaction. After I left, there was a violent reaction. It always happened in this manner. He was old and was eventually completely liberated, just in time to spend the last few weeks of his life with serenity.

One mother was distraught because of the anomalies that she noticed in her son. At times he would become enraged and would yell like a madman; he would blaspheme and, when he would calm down, could not remember anything about his behavior. He did not pray and would never agree to be blessed by a priest. One day, while the son was at work and, as usual, was wearing his mechanic's overalls, the mother asked that all his clothes be blessed, following the prayers of the *Ritual* (for exorcisms). When the unsuspecting son came back from work, he took off his dirty overalls and changed clothes. After a few seconds, he furiously tore the clothes off and put the dirty overalls back on. He never wore the blessed clothes, which he kept well away from the clothes that, he could tell, had not been blessed. This episode clearly demonstrated that the young man needed to be exorcised.

Two young brothers resorted to my blessings because they were vexed by health problems and strange noises in the house. These noises would occur mainly at set times during the night. Doing the blessings, I noticed some negative reactions, and I advised them to receive the sacraments frequently and to pray with intensity. I also encouraged them to use the three sacramentals (water, oil, and salt) and invited them to come back. When I questioned them, I found out that these incidents began when their parents decided to take their grandfather—who was all alone—into their house. The grandfather blasphemed constantly and cussed and cursed everyone and everything. Father Tomaselli, a now-deceased exorcist, used to say that at times a single blasphemer was sufficient to ruin an entire family with diabolical presences. This case proved his point.

The same demon can be present in more than one person. In this case, the demon who possessed Pina, a girl, said that he would leave her that night. Father Candido, although he knew that the demons almost always lie, asked other exorcists to help him, occasionally in the presence of a medical doctor. At times, to hold the girl still, they would lay her down on a long table. She would twist and turn and fall to the ground, but at the last moment, before hitting the floor, she slowed down, as though a hand was holding her up, and would never hurt herself. After working on her without any result all evening and half the night, the exorcists decided to quit. The next morning, Father Candido was exorcising a small boy, six or seven years old. The devil, from within that boy, began to mock the priest: "Last night you worked hard, but you did not gain anything. We won! And I was there too!"

Once, while exorcising a young girl, Father Candido asked the demon his name. "Zebulun", he answered.

When the exorcism was over, the priest sent the girl to pray in front of the tabernacle. When the next girl came to be exorcised, Father Candido asked this demon too for his name. The answer was the same: "Zebulun". The priest asked, "Are you the same demon who possessed the other girl? If you are, give me a sign. I command you, in the name of God, to go back to the girl you just left." The new girl uttered a sort of howl and then became quiet and appeared calm. In the meantime, the people who were in the room heard the girl who was praying at the tabernacle take up the same howl. Then Father Candido ordered, "Come here again." Immediately, the new girl began the same howling, and the other began to pray. In these cases, possession is obvious.

Possession is also evidenced by some profound answers, especially when given by children. Father Candido asked an eleven-year-old boy some tough questions after he became convinced of the presence of a demon. He asked, "On earth there are many great scientists, some very fine intellects, who deny the existence of God and your existence. What do you say to that?" And the boy immediately answered, "Those are not very fine intellects! They are very fine mediocrities!" And Father Candido added, referring to the demons, "There are others who knowingly deny God with their will. What do you call these?" The small possessed boy jumped up in fury. "Be careful. Remember that we wanted to reclaim our freedom even before him. We told him No forever." The exorcist continued, "Explain to me what is the meaning of reclaiming your freedom before God, when you are nothing if you are separated from him, just as I am nothing. It is as though, in the number ten, the zero wanted to be separated from the number one. What would it become? What would it accomplish? I command you, in the name of God: tell me what you achieved that is positive? Come on, speak!" The demon, full of anger and fear, would twist, drool, and sob in a horrible way, a way not possible for an eleven-year-old, and say, "Do not test me like this! Do not test me like this!" Many ask how we can be sure of speaking with the demons. In a case like this, there is no doubt.

Here is another case. One day Father Candido was exorcising a seventeen-year-old girl. She was a peasant who spoke the dialect of her town; her Italian was very poor. Two other priests were present for the exorcism. Once the presence of Satan was ascertained, these two continued to question her. Father Candido, while reciting the Latin prayers, began to add these Greek words: "Shut up! Quit it!" Immediately the girl turned toward him and said "Why are you commanding me to be quiet? Rather, tell that to these two who continue to ask questions!"

Many times, Father Candido questioned the demons in people of all ages; he, however, liked to tell about the questioning of children, because it was obvious that their answers were well beyond their age and therefore proved the certain presence of the devil.

One day Father Candido asked a thirteen-year-old girl, "Two enemies, who hated each other all their lives, hated each other to death, and both ended up in hell. What is the relationship that they will share now, since they will be with each other for all eternity?" And this was the answer: "How stupid you are! Down there everyone lives folded within himself and torn apart by his regrets. There is no relationship with anyone; everyone finds himself in the most profound solitude and desperately weeps for the evil that he has committed. It is like a cemetery."

THE FIRST "BLESSINGS"

With these "patients", it is profitable to use a euphemistic language. Therefore, we always call the exorcisms "blessings". The presence of the evil one, once it is ascertained, is referred to as "negativity". It is also advantageous that the prayers be said in Latin. All this is to avoid using words that alarm and thus obtain the opposite of what is desired. There are people who have the fixation of being possessed; in these cases, we can be almost certain that they are not. To someone in a confused state of mind, the fact of receiving an exorcism may become proof positive of possession, and nobody will ever be able to convince him differently. When I still do not know the person well, I insist on saying that I am blessing him, even if I am performing an exorcism; at times, I simply give the *Ritual*'s blessing for the sick.

The complete sacramental includes many introductory prayers followed by three true exorcisms. They are different and complementary and follow a logical succession toward liberation. It matters little that they were selected in 1614; it is a fact that they are the result of a direct and long experience. Alcuinus, who wrote them, tested them very well, balancing each sentence very carefully against the effect that they had on the devil-possessed. There are a few small omissions, which Father Candido and I corrected. For example, there is no mention of Mary. We added this to all three exorcisms, by using the words used by Pope Leo XIII in his exorcism. Since Alcuinus' exorcisms date back to the ninth and tenth centuries, these omissions are understandable.

I have already mentioned that an exorcism can last a few minutes or many hours. The first time that we exorcise someone, even if we realize right away that we are confronted by a "negativity", it is better to be brief. It is usually limited to a few introductory prayers and one of the three exorcisms; I usually choose the first, because it presents an opportunity for anointing. Although the *Ritual* does not mention this—and it does not mention many other things—experience taught us that the using of the oil of the catechumens while saying *"Sit nominis ti signo famulus tuus munitus"* is very effective. In doing this, we were inspired by the anointing during baptism. The demon tries to hide, not to be discovered, so as not to be expelled. Thus it happens that, at first, his presence is detected very little or not at all. As the exorcisms continue, however, their strength forces him to come out into the open. There are many ways to goad him, including anointing.

The *Ritual* does not specify the stance of the exorcist: some stand; some sit; some are at the right, some to the left of the possessed person, and some behind. The *Ritual* says only that, beginning with the words *"Ecce crucem Domini"* [Behold the Cross of the Lord], we should touch the neck of the patient with the hem of the stole, and the priest should hold his hand on his head. We have noticed that the demon is very sensitive to the five senses ("I enter through the senses", he told me once), and mostly through the eyes. Therefore we, Father Candido and his apprentices, hold two fingers on the eyes and raise the eyelids at specific times during the prayers. Almost always, in cases of evil presence, the eyes look completely white; we can barely discern, even with the help of both hands, whether the pupils are toward the top or the bottom of the eye.

The position of the pupils indicates the type of demons and troubles that are present. During questioning, we could always classify the types of demons according to a distinction inspired by chapter 9 of the book of Revelation.

The demons are very wary of talking; they must be forced to speak, and do so only in the most severe of cases, those of true and complete possession. When demons are voluntarily chatty it is a trick to distract the exorcist from his concentration and to avoid answering useful questions when they are interrogated. In our questions we must hold to the following rules of the *Ritual*: Never ask useless questions or out of curiosity. We must ask for the name, whether there are other demons and how many, when and how the evil one entered that particular body, and when he will leave. We must find out whether the presence of the demon is due to a spell, and the specifics of that spell. If the person ate or drank evil things, he must vomit them; if some sorcery was hidden, it is important to be told where it is hidden, so it can be burned with the appropriate cautions.

During an exorcism the evil one, if he is present, may emerge in slow stages or with sudden explosions. The exorcist's understanding of the strength and seriousness of the illness is progressive. Whether it is oppression, obsession, or possession; whether the evil is slight or deeply rooted, it is difficult to find texts that make clear distinctions. I use this measure: if a person, during an exorcism, enters completely into a trance, it is the demon who speaks through his mouth. If he moves, it is the demon who moves using his limbs; and if at the end of the exorcism the person does not remember anything, we have a case of *diabolical possession*: that is, the demon is inside the individual and from time to time acts through the body of the possessed. It is well to note that while during an exorcism the demon is forced—by the power of the rite—to come into the open, he can still attack the person at any other time, but usually in a less severe way.

If during an exorcism some reaction of the patient reveals a demonic attack, but consciousness remains, as well as some vague memory of words and actions, then we are in the presence of *diabolical oppression*. In this case, the demon is not always present in the body of an individual, but he attacks from time to time and causes physical and mental illness.

I will not speak much about the third form of attack besides possession and oppression, which is *diabolical obsession*. It consists of uncontrollable evil thoughts that torment an individual, especially at night, or sometimes always. In all cases the cure is the same: prayer, fasting, the sacraments, a Christian life, charity, and exorcisms. To identify a possible evil source we use some general, not foolproof, guidelines, because the "negativity", that is, the demons, tend to attack man in *five areas*. These attacks are more or less severe, according to their origin. The five areas are the following: *health, business, affections, enjoyment of life,* and *desire for death*.

Health. The evil one has the power to cause physical and mental illness. I have already mentioned that the two most commonly affected areas are the head and the stomach. Usually, the sickness is persistent. At times, though, it is transitory, lasting only the length of the exorcism. The latter include plague-like growths, stab wounds, and bruises. The *Ritual* suggests blessing the affected areas with the Sign of the Cross and sprinkling them with holy water.

Many times I have witnessed the efficacy of simply covering the area with the stole and pressing on it with one hand. Many times women have come to me before undergoing surgery for ovarian cysts, which were diagnosed following a sonogram and the description of the pain. After the benediction, the pain stopped; a new sonogram showed the absence of any cyst, and surgery was canceled.

Father Candido can document numerous cases of grave illnesses that disappeared simply with his "blessing", including medically verified brain tumors. I must caution that these incidents can happen only to people who are subject to "negativities", and by this I mean cases whose origin is of suspected evil origin.

Affections. The evil one can cause unrestrained animosities, especially toward those who love us the most. He destroys marriages, breaks up engagements; he fosters screaming fights in families where everyone truly loves one another, and always for futile reasons. Satan also ruins friendships; through his intervention, the victim feels unwelcome everywhere, avoided by everyone, ending in a desire for isolation. Then there follows a conviction of total lack of love and understanding, a complete affective void that makes marriage an impossibility. And so every time that a friendly relationship grows and blossoms into love, it suddenly ends, without reason.

Business. Impossibility to find work—even when it seems that a job offer is certain—for improbable, even absurd motives. The victim may finally have found a job but leaves it for no apparent reason and then searches for another job, but either does not go to the interview or leaves the new job as well, citing the same futile motive. The relatives of these unfortunate individuals suspect abnormal or irresponsible personality. I have witnessed extremely wealthy families fall into abject poverty for humanly unexplainable reasons. Successful industrialists are suddenly inexplicably faced with everything going to rack and ruin, or astute businessmen begin to make one bad decision after another and, as a result, fall seriously in debt. Yet again, owners of very popular stores experience a disastrous decrease in customers. When the evil one influences money matters, finding a job becomes impossible, the wealthy are suddenly forced into poverty, and the employed become jobless, and always without any apparent reason.

Enjoyment of life. Logically, physical illnesses, affective isolation, and economic bankruptcy bring about such pessimism that life is seen only in a negative way. Those so affected become incapable of optimism, of hope; life appears completely bleak, without any way out, unbearable.

Desire for death. The fifth stage. This is the final goal of the evil enemy: to bring us to despair and suicide. Here I immediately add that when we place ourselves under the protection of the Church, even if it is only with one exorcism, the fifth stage is eliminated. We seem to relive what Job was allowed to suffer: "Behold, he is in your power; only spare his life" (Job 2:6). I could tell many instances where, with almost miraculous intervention, the Lord saved some people from suicide.

I am sure that many readers identified with these five stages, with different degrees of intensity. I reiterate that most of the time all these ills have causes unrelated to evil intervention; we cannot, on our own, determine if one is possessed or oppressed by the evil one.

I will give two examples of the fifth, most serious, point, the desire to die and attempted suicide. I was dealing with a registered nurse who, due to a severe crisis, had the following desperate, illogical thought: "If I give this patient the wrong blood transfusion, I will be arrested, and I will be safely in prison." She followed through and put her plan into action; she was convinced she had injected the patient with the wrong blood type. She then went to her office, waiting to be arrested. As the hours went by, it became apparent that the transfusion had been successful, and the nurse repented of her action.

Giancarlo, a handsome young man, twenty-five years old, looked in perfect health and good spirits. However, he had a "tenant" who tormented him cruelly. Exorcisms gave him some relief, but not enough. One night he decided to end it all, as he had tried many other times. He walked along a busy section of railroad tracks, stopped at a wide curve, and lay down on the tracks in a sleeping bag. He remained there for four or five hours. Many trains went by in both directions, but each one traveled on the set of tracks opposite Giancarlo; for reasons that defy human understanding, they noticed him.

I asked Father Candido if, in his long experience as an exorcist, he had lost anyone whom he had blessed to suicide. He had lost one, and here is the story. A Roman girl who was in extremely poor condition due to total evil possession went to him to be exorcised. She began to feel some relief, even though she found it extremely difficult to fight the temptation to commit suicide. Her mother went to Father Candido one day; she believed that her daughter imagined her illness and kept rebuking her. Although Father Candido's explanations seemed to convince the woman, in reality it was not so. One day, when the daughter was confiding to her mother the torment of her constant temptation to suicide, this unworthy woman went into one of her usual tirades: "You are demented; you are worthless; you are not even able to kill yourself. Try it!"

and opened the window wide as she was saying this. The daughter jumped and died instantly. This is the only instance of a suicide among all those who went to Father Candido for exorcisms. However, it is more than evident that it was the fault of the mother, who was also responsible for the pitiful condition of her daughter.

I have mentioned that the length of time required for exorcisms is unpredictable. The active cooperation of the affected individual is very important. Nevertheless, even with the greatest collaboration, at times we can achieve only some improvement and not complete liberation. One day Father Candido was exorcising a great, big young man, the kind who makes an exorcist perspire, because he requires great physical efforts. It looked like a true fight. From the beginning, the young man told the priest, "I do not know if today is a good day for an exorcism; I have the feeling that I will hurt you." In fact, there ensued a real fight between the two, and the outcome was uncertain. All of a sudden the young man dropped to the floor, and Father Candido dropped on him exhausted. He told me, smiling, "If anyone had come into the room at that time, he would have been unable to distinguish the exorcist from the possessed." After a while the priest recovered and was able to finish the exorcism. Some days later Padre Pio sent the following warning to Father Candido: "Don't waste time and strength on that young man. It is all useless." With divine inspiration, Padre Pio knew that nothing would work with that particular young man. And the facts vindicated his intuition.

I add another observation: *"Diabolical possession is not a contagious disease, neither for the relatives nor for those who witness it, nor for the places in which exorcisms are held."* It is important to state this clearly, because often exorcists encounter great difficulties trying to find a place to exercise this sacramental. Many times we are refused access specifically because of the fear that the building will become "infested". It is necessary that priests, at least, become aware that the presence of anyone who is possessed and exorcisms practiced on them have no consequence on buildings or on those who live in them. We must instead fear sin; a hardened sinner, a blasphemer, can damage his family, his workplace, and everywhere he goes habitually.

Some instances that I have chosen not from among the most shocking but from the most common that happened to me follow.

Anna Maria, a sixteen-year-old girl, was distressed because she was failing school (in the past she had never had any difficulty studying), and at home she heard strange noises. She came to me with her parents and her sister. I blessed her and noticed negative signs. Then I blessed the mother, who was complaining of minor ailments. As I put my hands on her head, she let out a great scream and crumpled to the ground from the chair in which she was seated. I asked the two sisters to leave the room and continued with the exorcism with her husband's help. I noticed much stronger negative signs in the mother than in the girl. For Anna Maria three blessings were sufficient; it was a weak case of possession, and I was able to cure it right away. As for the mother, it required several months of weekly exorcisms. She recovered completely, much earlier than I had predicted after her reaction to the first blessing.

Giovanna, a thirty-year-old woman and mother of three sons, was sent to me by her confessor. She had headaches, fainting spells, and stomachaches. Doctors said she was completely well. Slowly, gradually, her illness appeared;

that is, she was possessed by three demons, who entered her through three different evil spells. The strongest spell was cast before her marriage, by a girl who wanted to marry her fiancé. Giovanna's family's strong prayer life greatly helped the exorcisms. Two of the demons left fairly quickly; the third proved more obstinate and required three years of weekly exorcisms before he left.

Marcella, a nineteen-year-old blond girl who appeared assured and defiant came to me for an appointment. She suffered piercing stomachaches, and both at home and at work she was unable to stop making offensive, sour comments. The doctors claimed she was perfectly healthy. As I put my hands on her eyes, at the beginning of the exorcism, her eyes were entirely white, and her pupils were barely discernible at the lower part of her eyes. She let out a sarcastic laugh. I barely had the time to think that I was dealing with Satan when I heard myself addressed thus: "I am Satan", with another bout of laughter. Little by little, Marcella intensified her prayer life, started receiving Communion and praying the Rosary daily, and went to confession weekly (confession is stronger than an exorcism!). She progressively improved and suffered setbacks only when she decreased the intensity of her prayers. She was healed after only two years.

Giuseppe, twenty-eight years old, came to me with his mother and sister. I realized immediately that he came to see me only to please his loved ones. He emanated a strong odor of smoke; he used and sold drugs and blasphemed. There was no point in talking about prayer and the sacraments. I tried to convince him to accept my exorcism, which, by necessity, was very brief, because the demon revealed himself immediately and violently. I had to stop. When I told Giuseppe that he was possessed he answered me, "I knew that already and I am happy; I get along fine with the devil." I never saw him again.

Sister Angela, although she was young, came to me in a truly pitiful physical condition; she could barely speak and certainly could not pray. Her entire body was in pain; there was almost no part of her that did not show some suffering. Her head would resound with internal blasphemies, and she also heard strange noises. The beginning of her troubles was a malediction (and possibly a spell) by an unworthy priest; Sister Angela offered all her suffering on behalf of her religious order. After many exorcisms, which proved beneficial, she was transferred to another city. I hope that she was able to find another exorcist to complete her liberation.

I will describe one among the many awful instances of spells cast on an entire family. The father, who was a very successful merchant, found himself suddenly and inexplicably without any sales. His warehouse was full of goods, but nobody came to buy anymore. Once, when he had been able to sell a large order, the truck that was supposed to deliver the merchandise broke down repeatedly and never reached its destination, and therefore the sale could not be completed. Another time, after great efforts, he was able to win a large contract. This time the truck arrived at the buyer's warehouse, but nobody was able to open the warehouse door, and once again the sale could not be completed. During the same period, a married daughter was abandoned by her husband, and the fiancé of another daughter left her on the eve of the wedding without any explanation. To this were added—as in most similar cases— health problems and strange noises. It was hard to say where to start. I recommended much prayer, frequent reception of the sacraments, and a truly Christian way of life; then I began exorcising all the members of the family. I also exorcised and celebrated the Holy Mass in the house and in the place of business of the father. After a year all this began to bear some fruit, and progress continued at a constant, even if slow, pace. These are truly trials of faith and perseverance!

Antonia, a twenty-year-old girl, came to me with her father, a baker. The daughter seemed to be a soothsayer. She heard strange voices, and she could not sleep or work. Almost at the same time, the father began suffering stomach pains that no medicine could help. When I blessed the daughter, I sensed a slightly negative presence. I told her that, unless I was mistaken, she needed only a few exorcisms. When I blessed the father, he went into a total trance; he remained silent and perfectly still. When he regained his senses, I realized that he had been totally unaware of what happened. I then cautioned the daughter not to say anything to him, to avoid scaring him, and asked them both to come back. At home the daughter was unable to keep silent and told her father everything. He became frightened and went to a sorcerer. The person who had advised them to come to me told me that they are both ill, but they have never come back to me. At times I run into persons who became discouraged by the slow pace of healing and turn to sorcerers for faster help, with disastrous consequences. God created us free; we are also free to ruin ourselves.

To conclude this chapter I would like to point out one thing: every exorcist has his own experiences that at times are unique. Some cases are so unusual that nobody else ever comes across them. I would not be surprised if some exorcists are perplexed by what I wrote, especially at the beginning of this chapter, concerning the position of the eyes, headaches, and stomachaches. These are phenomena that

Father Candido and all the exorcists that he trained encounter regularly, and they are real, whether any other exorcist has ever experienced them or not.

I believe that we must study with great respect different methodologies and experiences in exorcisms. Facts do not change, and the efficacy of a method cannot be discounted because the facts differ from someone else's experience.

THE DEMON'S BEHAVIOR

Generally the demon does all he can not to be discovered. He does not like to talk and tries everything to discourage both the exorcist and the possessed. Experience has taught me that this behavior follows four steps: prior to discovery, during exorcisms, at the beginning of liberation, and after liberation. I must caution that there are never two identical instances. The behavior of the evil one is most unpredictable and takes many different forms. What I am about to describe refers to the most frequently encountered behavior.

1. *Prior to discovery.* Demonic possession causes physical and mental disturbances. Therefore the possessed is usually under a doctor's care, and nobody suspects the true nature of the problems. Often doctors try to cure the symptoms for a lengthy period and try many drugs, always with very limited results. Commonly, the patient goes from doctor to doctor, accusing them of incompetence. Mental symptoms are the hardest to cure; many times the specialists find nothing wrong—although this also happens often with physical illness—and often the family accuses the possessed individual of imagining his problems. This is one of the heaviest crosses to bear for these "patients"; they are neither understood nor believed. Almost always, after fruitlessly searching for help from "official medicine", these individuals knock at the door of "healers" or, worse, sorcerers, seers, and witch doctors. In this manner, the problems increase.

Normally, anyone who comes to the exorcist (following a friend's suggestion; very rarely a priest's advice!) has already knocked at every doctor's door and is throughly sceptical; many times he has tried sorcerers and warlocks. Often an inexcusable lack of ecclesiastical care in this field is added to the lack of faith or the lack of practice in the faith of these individuals; the result is an understandable delay in turning to the exorcist.

We must remember that even in the cases of complete possession—that is, in cases when the demon is the one talking and acting, using the victim's body—the demon does not act consistently. He alternates periods of activity (usually called "moments of crisis") with unpredictable periods of rest. In this manner, with few exceptions, the person is able to function and hold a job or go to school in a seemingly normal manner. The person alone knows the tremendous effort that the performance of these tasks requires.

2. *During exorcisms*. At the beginning the demon tries his best to remain undetected or at least to hide the seriousness of his possession, even if he is not always successful. At times he is forced by the strength of the exorcism to reveal his presence at the first prayers; other times more sessions are required before he is discovered. I remember a young man who, at the first blessing, gave only a mild negative reaction. I thought, "This is an easy one; I will be done after this blessing and a few more." The second time, though, he became furious, and after that I could not begin an exorcism unless four strong men were present to subdue him.

On other occasions, one must wait for the "hour of God". I clearly remember one person who had consulted several exorcists, including myself, without any indication of an evil presence. Finally, one time the demon was forced to reveal himself, and after that the exorcisms proceeded fruitfully. Sometimes, from the first or second blessing the demon reveals all his strength, which changes from person to person. At times the revelation is progressive; some possessed appear to have a different sickness at each session, giving the impression that every ill in the body must be brought out one at a time in order to be healed.

The demon reacts in various manners to prayers and injunctions. Many times he tries to appear indifferent; in reality he suffers and continues to suffer increasingly until liberation is achieved. Some possessed individuals are silent and immobile, and, if provoked, any reaction is limited to the eyes. Others fling themselves about, and unless they are held down, they harm themselves. Others wail, especially if a stole is pressed to the affected parts of their bodies, as the *Ritual* suggests, or if they are blessed with the Sign of the Cross or with holy water. Very few are violent, and these must be held tightly by those who are helping the exorcist or by their relatives.

Demons are very reluctant to speak. The *Ritual*, very rightly, admonishes the exorcist not to ask questions out of curiosity, but to ask only what is useful for liberation. The first thing that must be asked is the name. For the demon, who is so reluctant to reveal himself, revealing himself is a defeat; even when he has revealed his name, he is always reluctant to repeat it, even during following exorcisms. Then we command the evil one to tell how many demons are present in a particular body. There can be many or few, but there is always one chief, and he is always the first to be named. When the demon has a biblical name or one given in tradition (for example, Satan, Beelzebub, Lucifer, Zebulun, Meridian, Asmodeus), we are dealing with "heavyweights", tougher to defeat. The degree of difficulty is also relative to the intensity with which the demon possesses a person. When several demons are present, the chief is always the last to leave.

The strength of possession is manifested also from the reaction of the demon to holy names. Generally the evil one does not and cannot say those names; he substitutes expressions such as "he" (referring to God or Jesus) or "she" (referring to our Lady). Other times he says, "your Boss" or "your Lady", to indicate Jesus or Mary. If the possession is very strong and the demon is high ranking (I repeat that demons keep the rank that they held when they were angels, such as thrones, principalities, or dominions), then it is possible for him to say the name of God and Mary, always followed by horrible blasphemies.

Some believe, I know not why, that demons are talkative and that, if they are present during an exorcism, the demon will publicly denounce all their sins. It is a false belief; demons are reluctant to speak, and when they talk, they say silly things to distract the exorcist and escape his questions. There are exceptions. One day Father Candido invited a priest who prided himself on his scepticism to be present during an exorcism. The priest accepted the invitation, but his behavior was disparaging; he stood with his arms crossed, without praying—as all who are present should do—and with an ironic smile. At one point, the demon turned to him, saying, "You say that you do not believe I exist. But you believe in women; yes, you believe in women, and how!" That poor unfortunate priest, quietly and walking backward, reached the door and quickly disappeared.

Another time the demon disclosed sins to discourage the exorcist. Father Candido was exorcising a handsome young man who was possessed by a great beast of a demon. Trying to discourage the exorcist, the demon said: "Can't you see that you are wasting your time? This one never prays. He goes around with . . . and does . . ." and there followed a long list of ugly sins. At the end of the exorcism, Father Candido fruitlessly tried to convince that young man to make a general confession. It was necessary almost to drag him into the confessional, where he hastened to say that he had no sins to confess. Then Father Candido asked, "But did you not do this and such?" Dumbfounded, the poor man was forced to admit his transgressions. As the confessor continued with the list of sins, the young man admitted every one of the facts revealed by the demon. After receiving absolution, the young man left, mumbling, "I don't understand anything anymore! These priests know everything!"

The *Ritual* suggests asking other questions dealing with the length of time of possession, the motive, and similar topics. I will mention later how we must behave in case of spells and what questions to ask. Let us not forget that the demon is the prince of lies. He freely accuses one person or another to foster suspicion and enmity; his answers must be sifted carefully. I will say only that generally questioning the demons is not of great importance. For instance, often when the demon sees he is losing strength, he gives one date as the day of his departure but then lingers on. An experienced exorcist such as Father Candido was often able to guess not only what kind of demon he was dealing with but also often even his name; therefore he did not ask too many questions. At times, however, he would ask the demon's name only to be told, "You know it already!" Which was true.

In cases of strong possessions the demon might speak voluntarily to discourage the exorcist. Many times I was told, "You cannot do anything against me!" "This is my home; I am happy here, and here I will stay." "You are wasting your time." Other times I was threatened: "I will eat your heart!" "Tonight I will frighten you so much that you will not be able to close your eyes." "I will come into your bed like a snake." "I will throw you out of bed." Then, confronted with my answers, he would fall silent. For instance, when I say, "I am enveloped within the mantle of our Lady. What can you do to me?" or "The Archangel Gabriel is my protector; try and fight him!" or "My guardian angel watches over me so that I won't be touched; you cannot harm me", the demon remains silent.

The exorcist is always able to find a particularly weak spot. Some demons cannot bear to have the Sign of the Cross traced with a stole on an aching part of the body; some cannot stand a puff of breath on the face; others resist with all their strength against blessing with holy water. Then there are certain sentences within the prayers of exorcism to which the demon reacts with violence or by losing strength. At this point, as the *Ritual* suggests, the exorcist will repeat those sentences. The session's duration varies according to the judgment of the priest. Often the presence of a doctor is useful not only to give the initial diagnosis but also to help determine the length of the exorcism. When the obsessed or the exorcist is feeling poorly, the doctor is the one who advises when to end the session. The exorcist also is able to determine when it is useless to go any farther.

3. *Nearing the exit of the demon*. This is a delicate and difficult moment, which could also take a long time. Sometimes the demon indicates that he has lost strength, but in other circumstances he tries to launch the last attacks. In the case of a common sickness, we often notice that the patient pro-

gresses gradually until he is well again. In the case of possession, on the other hand, most frequently the opposite happens; the individual often feels increasingly worse, and when he cannot stand it any longer he is healed.

For a demon, to leave a body and go back to hell—where he is almost always condemned—means to die forever and to lose any ability to molest people actively. He expresses this desperation during exorcisms with words such as these: "I am dying, I am dying!" "I can't take it any longer." "Enough, you are killing me!" "You are murderers, hangmen. All priests are murderers!" And similar sentences. Whereas at the beginning of the exorcisms he would say, "You cannot do anything to me"; now he says, "You are killing me; you have won." At the beginning he would say that he would never leave, because he was perfectly happy in a particular body; now he claims he feels ill and wants to leave. It is a fact that every exorcism is like hitting the demon with a bat. He suffers greatly; at the same time he also causes pain and weakness to the person he possesses. He even admits that he is better off in hell than during an exorcism. One time, while Father Candido was exorcising one person close to liberation, the demon openly told him, "Do you think that I would leave if this were not worse than the suffering of hell?" Exorcisms had become truly unbearable to him.

We must keep something else in mind to help the person who is nearing his liberation; the demon tries to communicate his feelings to the possessed. The demon can't take it any longer, and he communicates this condition of desperation to his victim; he feels near the end of his life, unable to reason rationally, and transmits the same feeling of madness and of near death to the possessed. How often these people beg me, "Tell me truly, am I crazy?"

Exorcisms become more difficult also for the victim, and if someone does not almost force him to keep the appointment he will not go. At times individuals who were near or very near liberation stopped coming to their appointments altogether. These "patients" must often be helped to pray and to go to church because they cannot do it on their own. They also need help undergoing exorcisms. They must constantly be encouraged, especially during the final stages.

Undoubtedly the length of time required before liberation contributes to the discouragement and to the physical exhaustion. The victim feels that his ills are incurable. Sometimes the demon may also cause real sickness, physical but primarily psychological, that must be medically treated after liberation. At other times the healing is complete and requires nothing more.

4. *After liberation*. It is very important not to decrease prayer, the reception of sacraments, and living a Christian life. An occasional exorcism is also beneficial because it is not unusual for the demon to repeat his attacks, trying to come back; it is well not to give him any openings. We may call this a period of gathering strength to safeguard a successful liberation. Occasionally some of my "patients" have experienced relapses. When there was no negligence involved, that is, he had maintained an intense spiritual life, the second liberation was easy. However, when the relapse was helped by lack of prayer or, even worse, by falling into habitual sin, the possession was worse than before, just as Matthew 12:43–45 describes. The demon comes back with seven more worse than himself.

I am sure that by now the reader realizes that the demon tries his best to hide his presence. This is one of the facts that helps to differentiate demonic possession from some psychological problems. In the latter instance usually the patient does his best to attract attention. Conversely, the demon acts very carefully.

A VICTIM'S WITNESS

This chapter is a clearly written witness by someone who was once possessed. It is difficult even for an experienced exorcist to understand what the obsessed feel. What may appear as an infestation of average intensity hides such suffering that the patient himself can hardly describe it. One victim, G. G. M., made every effort to express the inexpressible, trusting primarily in the understanding of those who are afflicted by the same torment.

It all started at sixteen. Before then, I was a happy youth. I was open, quite good humored, even if some sort of oppression appeared to pursue me. My friends would tell me, "We do this and such; why not you?" Or, "We are going to that place; why not you?" I could not understand why, but I did not make an issue of it. I lived in a coastal town; the sea, the dawn, and the fields were of great help to avoid becoming melancholy. After my sixteenth birthday I moved to Rome, I left the Church, and I began to pursue all the pleasures that a large city offers to a newcomer. That is, I began to experience all those excesses that are completely unknown in a small town. Pretty soon I became familiar with the homeless, drug addicts, thieves, "easy" girls, and so on. I was in a hurry to take in all the "noise" that was distracting me from the peace that I had known before. The new dimension in which I began to immerse myself was artificial, bloated, nauseating.

My father was oppressive. He controlled my every move and was always disgusted with me. The result of his disgust and of the humiliations to which he subjected me pushed me out into the streets. I left home and became intimately acquainted with hunger, cold, sleep, and meanness. I cultivated easy women and hard friends. Soon I found myself asking unanswerable questions such as, "Why do I live? Why am I in the middle of the street? Why am I like this while others have the strength to work and smile?"

At that time I lived with a girl who believed that evil was stronger than good. She talked of witches and sorcerers; her writings were mind boggling. I thought that she was very intelligent because her writings on the world and on life were beyond the human realm. I read all of her manuscripts, and then I forced her to burn them all in front of me. Because they spoke only of evil, I was afraid to keep them around the house. She hated me for it, and I did not understand why; I tried to help her exit that black hole, but I failed. She would deride me and the goodness that I tried to promote.

I went back to live with my parents, but I started dating a girl who was worse than the first one. For a few years I was despondent, unlucky, and persecuted by all who knew me. It seemed that I was surrounded by darkness; all smiles had left me, and tears were always ready to fall. I was desperate, and I asked myself again, "Why am I alive? Who am I? Why is man on earth?" Naturally, my circle of friends was not interested in these questions, and in a moment of extreme desperation I cried with a thread of sound, "My God, I am finished! I am here in front of you. Help me!" It looked as though I had been heard, because a few days later my girlfriend went into a church, received Communion, and converted in record time.

Not to be outdone, I did the same. I happened to walk into a church during the procession of Our Lady of

Lourdes. I was asked to help to carry the statue, and, although I was embarrassed, I accepted, and then I was proud of this honor. I received Communion, and I was surprised by the confessor, who was kind and understanding. I left the church telling myself, "I made it; I came back to goodness." Even though I did not know what goodness was, I felt that I had found it. Some weeks later I heard about Medjugorje, where our Lady had been appearing since 1981. My girlfriend and I left immediately, pushed by a wonder that I cannot describe. We came back fully to the Church. We loved God more than ourselves; she became a nun, and I contemplated the priesthood. I was so happy to have a motive to live and to believe in eternal life that I could not contain my joy.

Unfortunately, this was only the beginning. "Someone" was not happy with my new life. A few years later I went back to Medjugorje, and, when I came back to Rome, I heard the echo of the same blackness in which my soul had lived before I discovered God. In a matter of weeks this sensation became reality. I had attributed it to my father's oppression, to the hard life that I lived, and to a torment that I mistakenly believed was shared by all. I started to suffer as I had never done before. I was perspiring, I was feverish, and I had no strength left. I could not eat by myself and had to be spoon-fed. I felt that I was suffering with something other than my body; in fact, I felt that my body was a stranger. I was prey to the strongest despair, and I saw, I know not with whose eyes, a terrible darkness that was not part of the room in which I was or of the bed in which I had lain for months. This darkness was engulfing my future, my ability to live, and any hope of tomorrow. It was as though I were being killed by an unseen knife, and I felt that whoever was pressing this knife hated me and wanted something more than my death. It is very difficult to put my feelings into words, but I am explaining exactly what I felt.

After several months I became crazy. I could no longer reason, and those around me wanted to take me to an insane asylum. I could no longer understand what I was saying because I was living in another dimension, a place in which I was suffering. Reality appeared detached from me. It was as though I were present in time only with my body, but my soul was somewhere else, in a horrible place where no light can penetrate and where there is no hope.

For many months I remained between life and death, and I was unable to think anymore. I lost friends, relatives, and my family's understanding. I was outside the world; they were unable to understand me, nor could I demand that they try, because I knew what I felt inside, and I knew I could never describe it. I almost entirely forgot the things of God, even if I kept turning to him with tears and unending complaints. I felt that he was far away, a distance that I could measure not in miles but in denials. That is, something inside me kept saying "No" to him, to goodness, to life, to me. I thought about turning to a hospital for help because I thought that the fever that had not left me in months had some physical origin. If I could cure my body I would feel better; I had to do something.

No hospital in Rome would accept me just because I had a fever. I had to travel two hundred miles before any hospital would take me. I was there twenty days, and I underwent every known test and examination. I was dismissed with a bill of health that could have been the envy of every athlete. I was as healthy as a horse, but an addendum noted that nobody could explain my fever and the condition of my face, which was bloated and corpselike.

I was as white as a sheet of paper. As soon as I left the hospital, where my symptoms had subsided somewhat, I fell prey to a very severe crisis. I vomited many times. I suffered all that is possible for a man to suffer, and I found myself in an unknown part of the city. I do not know how I arrived there. My legs moved on their own; my arms and my body were totally independent from my will. It was a horrible feeling; I would tell my body what to do, and it would not obey me; I do not wish this experience on anyone. As if all this were not sufficient, the darkness came back; this time it engulfed not only my soul but also my body. I saw everything as though it were the middle of the night, even during the middle of the day. My suffering had become unbelievable. I began to scream, to twist on the ground as though I were on fire, and I kept pleading with Mary, crying, "Mother, Mother, have mercy on me. Mother, I beg you! Mother mine, have mercy on me because I am dying!" My pain did not diminish, and my suffering was so extreme that I lost all sense of direction. Leaning on the walls in the street, I reached a telephone booth. I was finally able to dial a number, hitting the glass and the walls of the booth all the while. The only person whom I knew in that town came to pick me up and drive me back to Rome. Before my acquaintance came, I had a flash of sanity, and I understood that I had seen hell. I did not touch it or actually enter it; I simply had seen it from a distance. That experience changed my life more than my pilgrimage to Medjugorje had.

I still tried to explain away my condition as a psychological problem; I had not thought of extrasensorial causes. I tried to explain it as a result of an oppressive father, childhood traumas, emotional shocks, maladjustments, and other reasons. By adding all these factors, I came up with my current condition. I had studied psychology for five years on my own, and I thought I had reached a diagnosis to justify my pain. A friar advised me to call a charismatic minister who had the gift of knowledge and operated under strict guidance of a bishop. Since this advice was given to me on the feast day of Our Lady of Good Counsel, I acted on it. This charismatic told me, "Someone cast a death spell on you. Eight months ago you ate of an evil fruit." I burst into laughter and disbelieved him completely. Later, as I started reflecting on his words, I began to nurture some hope. It was a feeling I had all but forgotten, and I started thinking back eight months. "It is true", I told myself, "I really ate of that fruit." I remembered that I did not want to eat it, because I felt an instinctive revulsion against the person who had offered it to me. As everything fell into place, I followed the advice I had been given, which was "be exorcised."

I began looking for an exorcist. During my quest, priests and bishops laughed at me and subjected me to humiliations; here I discovered a facet of the Church that had been distorted by her own pastors. Finally I landed at Father Amorth's door. I remember the day very well. I did not yet know what a "particular blessing" was. I thought it was the Sign of the Cross that the priest traces after Mass. I sat down, and Father Amorth put his stole around my shoulders and one hand on my head. He began to pray in Latin, but I did not understand a word he said. After a while I felt a cold, almost frozen, dew fall on my head and on the rest of my body. My fever left me for the first time in almost one year. I said nothing. Father continued, and, little by little, hope began to live in me. The light of day was returning, the song of the birds ceased to sound like the cawing of crows, and the noises around me were not obsessive anymore; they were simply noises. Until then I had lived with earplugs, because the smallest sound caused me to jump.

Father Amorth told me to come back, and as soon as I left I felt an overwhelming desire to smile, to sing, to be joyful. "How wonderful", I told myself, "it is over!" It is true, I felt all that I described, all my pain, had been caused by the rage of "someone" who hated me, and I was not crazy. "It is true", I kept repeating to myself in the car, "it is all true." Today, three years later, one exorcism after another, I am normal again. I have discovered that happiness comes from God and not from our victories and our efforts.

After a simple exorcism, evil, so-called misfortune, melancholy, anguish, jerkiness in the legs, tense nerves, insomnia, the fear of being schizophrenic or epileptic (I had fallen a few times), and many other signs of illness disappeared. Three years have gone by, and I have proof that demonstrates—to myself only, of course—that demons exist, and that they are much more active than we think. They do everything not to be found out. They even convince us that we have this or the other illness, while all along it is they who are the authors of all evil. However, they tremble in front of a priest with an aspergillum in his hands.

I decided to put my experience in writing to alert the readers. While I unfortunately experienced the wickedness of evil to the fullest, none of us can ignore this aspect of our lives. In retrospect I am glad that God allowed me to undergo such a severe trial, because I am now beginning to reap the fruits of so much suffering. My soul has been purified, and I see what I could not see before. Above all, I am less sceptical and more aware of the reality that surrounds me. I thought that God had abandoned me; now I realize that it was at that very moment that he was molding me to be ready to meet him.

I also want to encourage those who have the same sickness; do not lose heart. I caution you not to believe the evidence of your eyes. Do not believe that God abandons you, even if all the evidence points to it; it is not true. When all is said and done, you will have proof that God was with you. All you have to do is persevere, even if it takes years. I also believe that the power of exorcisms comes from God and not from the will of the exorcist or the patient. It is my experience that the efficacy of the exorcism is more directly related to the willingness to convert of the patient than to the exorcism itself. Confession and Communion are worth as much as a strong exorcism. After a good confession, the torments that I described above disappeared immediately. In Communion I felt a sweetness that I did not believe could exist.

Years ago, before all my sufferings, I went to confession and received Communion. Since I was not suffering, I did not realize that these practices were a form of immunization from evil. Now I know it, and I invite everyone, but above all the lukewarm, to believe that God is truly present at the door of the confessional and in that Host we so often take so casually.

I also want to invite the sceptics to *believe*, before "someone" helps you against your will. Finally, I turn to the poor obsessed individuals—nobody is poorer than they are. They are hated by Satan, who uses their own friends and acquaintances to kill them or oppress them. I exhort you, do not lose your faith; do not reject hope. Do not allow your wills to be subjected to violent suggestions or the ghosts that the evil one presents to you.

Satan's true goal is not to make you suffer or to harm you. He does not seek our pain but something more. He wants our defeated soul to say, "Enough. I am defeated; I am a piece of clay in the hands of evil. God cannot liberate me. God forgets his children if he allows such suffering. God does not love me; evil is greater than he is." This is the true victory of evil. We must rebuke it even if we no longer have faith because our pain dulls it. "We must want faith." The devil cannot touch our will. Our will does not belong to God or to the devil; it is ours alone because God gave it to us when he created us. We must always say "No" to those who want to destroy it. We must believe, like Saint Paul, that "in the name of Jesus Christ every knee must bend in the heavens, on earth, and under the earth."

This is our salvation. If we do not firmly believe, the evil that was forced on us—whether with spells or curses—can last for years without any improvement. I also want to reassure those who believe they are crazy and do not believe that there is a remedy to their plight. I can witness that, after many exorcisms, this evil goes away as though it had never existed. Therefore we must not fear it but praise God for the cross that he gives us to bear. After the cross, there is always the resurrection, just as after the night the day always comes; everything has been created thus. God does not lie, and we have been chosen to walk with Jesus Christ at Gethsemane; we keep him company in his suffering in order to be resurrected with him.

I offer my testimony to Mary Immaculate. I hope that, under her guidance, it may be of help to my brethren in pain. To all those who have been used as instruments of the devil to bring about the martyrdom that I suffered, I answer with love, pardon, smiles, and blessings. I pray that my pain will guide them to the light that I have freely received from our marvelous God.

G. G. M.

EFFECT OF EXORCISMS

When a person is subject to "negativities"—that is, some form of evil influence—we often notice improvement after an exorcism, even when the evil presence did not manifest itself during the session. When we try to determine whether there is a demonic presence, the reactions of the day of the exorcism itself are not conclusive. For instance, it does not matter if on the day of the exorcism the person shows signs of improvement or deterioration, sleepiness or grogginess, appearance of bruises or disappearance of pain. What is important is what happens on the subsequent days. Usually nothing changes the first couple of days; then signs of improvement begin to appear over a length of time that can last from a few to many days, according to the gravity of the illness. If no improvement is noted for several days, and no signs of "negativities" appeared during the exorcism, it generally means that the source of the problem is not of demonic origin. If the exorcist suspects that the demon is hiding, he can advise another blessing.

What is important is the demeanor of the patient during the following sessions and as a consequence of the exorcism. It may be that the evil influence showed all its strength—whether slight or serious—on the first day. On other occasions it seems that the demon tries to hide, and his power gradually emerges over several sessions. Finally the power slowly weakens. I remember a young man who showed very little negativity at first; during the second exorcism he began to scream and thrash about. Although his condition was worse than many others, it required only a few months of exorcisms before he was liberated.

The cooperation of the patient is fundamental for success. I always say that the exorcism is 10 percent of the cure; the remaining 90 percent is the responsibility of the individual. What does this mean? It means that there is a need for much prayer, frequent reception of the sacraments, living a life according to the Gospel, using sacramentals (I will discuss later the use of exorcised water, salt, and oil). It also means asking others to pray for a cure—the prayer of the entire family, parish or religious communities, prayer groups, etc., is especially fruitful—and requesting many Masses. Pilgrimages and charitable works are also useful. Above all, liberation is obtained through abundant personal prayer and through it a union with God that becomes a way of life. Many times I must deal with people who are far from religious practices. I have found that active participation in the parish or in prayer groups, especially renewal groups, is extremely beneficial.

I often compare demonic possession with drugs to demonstrate my point about cooperation. Everyone is familiar with drug addiction; everyone knows that the addict can be cured, but on two conditions. First, he must be helped by joining a support group or other similar organization because he cannot do it alone. Second, he also must actively cooperate by his own personal effort; otherwise every form of help is useless. In the case of evil influence, I have already indicated the personal help. While the direct fruits of exorcisms and liberation are slow, I have seen the indirect results—that is, conversion—happen very rapidly. Entire families become committed to intensely lived Christian practices and become united in prayer—very often through the Rosary. I have witnessed how true generosity has overcome obstacles to healing, such as an irregular marriage situation or the inability to forgive wrongs or be reconciled with a particular person, mostly close relatives, with whom every communication had been broken.

One of the most effective tools against evil influences is one of the hardest Gospel precepts: forgive your enemies. In this case the enemy is usually the person who cast the spell and who keeps it going. Sincere forgiveness, which includes prayer on that person's behalf and having Masses said for the person's conversion, often breaks open a deadlocked situation and helps speed up healing.

Benefits of exorcisms include healing from ills and sicknesses that at times appear incurable. We may be dealing with inexplicable pain in different parts of the body—I repeat that the most frequently affected parts are the head or the stomach. Or we may be faced with a specific illness, clearly diagnosed by a doctor who was either unable to cure it or who declared it incurable. Demons have the power to provoke sickness. The Gospel tells us of a woman who had been bent by a demon for eighteen years—could this have been a spinal deformation?—and was healed when Jesus expelled the demon. Similarly, he liberated a man who was deaf and mute through evil influence. Jesus also healed people who were deaf and mute because of an illness that was unrelated to satanic influence. The Gospel makes very precise distinctions between those who are ill and those who are possessed, even when the symptoms are identical.

Who is most seriously afflicted? Who is the hardest to cure? According to my personal experience, the hardest to cure are the victims of the most powerful spells. I remember some people who had been subjected to a spell in Brazil called *macumbe*. I exorcised others who had been afflicted by African witch doctors. All were extremely hard to heal. Other tough cases involve spells that are cast on entire families to destroy them. Sometimes the problem is so complex that I do not know where to start. It takes a long time to liberate people who are periodically struck by new spells. The exorcism is stronger than the spell; therefore the healing cannot be blocked, but it can be slowed down for a long time.

Who is the most afflicted? Without a doubt, it is the young. When I think back to the causes of evil possession and review those occasions that invite the evil one to interfere with someone, it becomes obvious that in today's environment the young are the most at risk. This is because the young lack faith and ideals; therefore they are those most exposed to disastrous experiences. Even children are very vulnerable, not because of personal fault, but because of their weakness. Many times when we exorcise an adult we discover that the demonic presence can be traced to early childhood, or even worse, to the moment of birth or even to their gestation.

Several times I have been told that I exorcise more women than men. This is true for all exorcists. It is not a mistake to think that women are more exposed to evil attacks than men. Men and women are not exposed in the same manner. It is also true that women are much more inclined than men to turn to an exorcist for a "blessing". Many men, even if they are certain that they have been struck, absolutely refuse to go near a priest. I have also asked more men than women to change their lives, and they have refused. These men have never returned, even though they were fully conscious of their affliction. The biggest obstacle to healing is the refusal to convert from practicing atheism to a life of faith, or from a life of sin to a life of grace.

I do not deny that *to be healed from this evil requires great efforts to live an intensely Christian life*. I am also convinced that this is one of the reasons why God allows this evil. Many are the times that victims of satanic influence told me that their faith was extremely lukewarm, and their prayer life was almost nonexistent. They confessed that drawing closer to God—sometimes with great zeal—was a direct result of the evil that had afflicted them. While we are attached to this life and to this earth much more than we realize, the Lord is looking much farther; he looks to our eternal good.

In the meantime, the exorcist goes on with his blessings and does not limit his efforts to encouraging the patient to pray and to pursue all those forms of religious life that we have already mentioned. He will also endeavor to irritate, debilitate, and weaken the demon with every tool available to him. The *Ritual* advises the exorcist to insist on the blessings that cause the demon to react: these change from person to person and from time to time. Some cannot stand being sprinkled with holy water; others become exasperated if we blow on them. (Tertullian tells us that this practice has been used since the times of the Fathers.) Others cannot bear the smell of incense; therefore it is beneficial to use it. Still others experience pain when the organ plays and at the sound of sacred music and Gregorian chant. These are all helpful means whose efficacy I have experienced firsthand.

How does the demon behave as the exorcism progresses? I will repeat what I have already said. The demon suffers and causes suffering. The pain that he experiences during an exorcism is unimaginable for us. One day Father Candido asked a demon if there is fire in hell, a fire that burns hot. The demon answered, "If you knew what fire you are for me, you would not ask me this question." Obviously we are not talking about material fire, which is caused by flammable material. We witness how the demon burns when he comes in contact with sacred items such as crucifixes, reliquaries, and holy water.

I have also heard demons tell me many times that they suffer more during exorcisms than in hell. When I ask, "Why don't you go to hell, then?" they answer, "Because we are only interested in making this person suffer." Here we see clearly the diabolical wickedness: the devil knows that he cannot possibly benefit from the suffering that he causes. On the contrary, he knows that his eternal punishment will increase. Even so, even at the cost of his own suffering, he cannot stop causing evil simply for evil's sake.

Even the names of the demons, as in the case of angels, tell us their function. The most important demons have biblical names or names transmitted to us by tradition: Satan or Beelzebub, Lucifer, Asmodeus, Meridian, Zebulun. Other names more clearly tell us the purpose of their actions—Destruction, Perdition, Ruin—or they indicate individual evils—Insomnia, Terror, Discord, Envy, Jealousy, Sloth.

In the majority of cases, when they leave a soul they are destined to go to hell; at times they are freed in the desert (I refer you to the book of Tobit, where we see Asmodeus chained in the desert by the Archangel Raphael). I always force them to go at the foot of the Cross, to receive their sentence from Jesus Christ, who is the sole judge.

WATER, OIL, SALT

Among the means that exorcists (and not only exorcists) commonly use I mention first *exorcised water* (or at least holy water), *exorcised oil* (olive), and *exorcised salt*. Every priest can recite the prayers of the *Ritual* to exorcise those three items; he does not need special permission. Rather, *it is very useful to be aware of the specific use of these three sacramentals*, which, if used with faith, are greatly beneficial.

Exorcised water. Blessed water is already widely used in all liturgical rites. Its importance reminds us immediately of baptism. During the prayer of blessing with exorcised water we ask the Lord that, through aspersion with water, he will grant us the following three benefits: forgiveness of sins, defense from the wickedness of the evil one, and the gift of divine protection. (In Italy, when we want to give an example of two things that are incompatible, we say that "they are as compatible as the devil and holy water.") The prayer continues by mentioning other effects of exorcised water. Besides delivering from the demons, such as healing from illness, it also increases divine graces and protects houses and all the dwellings in which the faithful live from every evil influence caused by the wickedness of Satan. The *Ritual* also lists protection against every insidiousness of the infernal enemy and from every presence that could be harmful to the well-being or the peace of anyone living on the premises, granting them health and serenity.

Exorcised oil. If used in faith, this oil helps to dispel the power of demons, their attacks, and the ghosts that they evoke. It is also beneficial to the health of mind and body. It is well to recall the ancient tradition of anointing wounds with oil, and the power that Jesus gave his apostles of healing the sick by imposition of hands and anointing with oil. There is one property that is particular to exorcised oil: that of separating impurities from the body. Many times I have blessed people who were subject to spells cast as a result of eating or drinking something cursed. It is easy to find out if this is the case because the stomachache that follows is very characteristic. At times symptoms of this spell include peculiar burps, explosive hiccups, or growls, especially during religious practices such as going to church, during prayer time, and, most frequently, during exorcisms. In these circumstances the body must expel whatever evil substances it has taken. Exorcised oil is very helpful in separating the body from these impurities. Drinking blessed water can also be used.

At this point, anyone who is not familiar with or has never seen these objects will find it hard to believe what I just said; therefore I must be more specific. What are we expelling? At times it is dense and foamy saliva or a sort of white and grainy pap. Other times we find the strangest objects, such as nails, pieces of glass, small wooden dolls, knotted strings, rolled wire, cotton thread of different colors, or blood clots. These objects may be expelled naturally, often by vomiting. I want to point out that the body is never harmed, even by sharp glass; on the contrary, it receives great benefit. Father Candido used to keep a basket of such objects that were expelled from different people. Sometimes the means of expulsion remains a mystery. For example, the victim feels a stomach pain as if caused by a nail; then he finds a nail on the floor near him, and the pain disappears. What is most strange is that all these objects materialize the very instant in which they are expelled. During an interview, Father Candido stated, "I saw pieces of glass, iron, hair, and bone being vomited, or small plastic objects, shaped—or with the head shaped—as a cat, lion, or serpent. Surely these strange objects are connected with the cause of demonic possession."

Exorcising salt too is beneficial for expelling demons and for healing soul and body. The specific function of this salt is to protect places from an evil presence or influence. When there is suspicion of evil infestation, I usually advise people to place exorcised salt across the threshold and in the four corners of the room or rooms that are affected.

The "unbelieving Catholic world" may laugh at my assertions. It is certain that sacramentals are most efficacious when they are used in faith; without faith, they are ineffective. Vatican II and the Code of Canon Law (canon 1166) use the same words to define sacramentals as "sacred signs by which spiritual effects especially are signified and are obtained by the intercession of the Church". Whoever uses these tools with faith obtains unhoped-for results. I know of many illnesses that resisted every medicine but disappeared after I simply traced the Sign of the Cross with exorcised oil over the affected part.

Blessed incense is also effective for houses; this topic will be treated separately. Incense has always been considered an antidote against evil spirits, even among pagan civilizations, as well as an element used to praise and adore divinities. Liturgical use of incense has been curtailed in our times, but it remains an efficacious element of praise to God and of battle against evil.

The *Ritual* includes a special blessing over *clothing*. Many times I have witnessed its efficacy on people who were under an evil influence. Other times I have used it as a test to determine the presence of evil. Many times I have been approached by people (parents, fiancées, etc.) who questioned whether a loved one was under the influence of a demon. If such a loved one does not believe in evil presences, usually he or she is devoid of any religious faith and has no intention of going to a priest to be blessed. What can be done in this situation? Usually, after I bless some items of clothing, they are put back in the closet of the affected individual. Many times the victim tears off the blessed clothes as soon as he puts them on, because their touch is unbearable. I have already given an example of this. Blessed water is another test. For example, a mother who suspects an evil presence in a son or husband uses blessed water to cook some soup or to brew coffee or tea. Often the affected person finds that particular food bitter and inedible, without understanding why.

I caution that these tests are a positive indication of possession: that is, if a person is sensitive to blessed water or clothes, it may be a sign of an evil presence. I cannot make the opposite statement. In other words, if there is no reaction to these tests, it does not necessarily mean the absence of an evil presence. Demons go to any length to avoid detection.

They try to hide during an exorcism as well; rightly the *Ritual* cautions the exorcist against diabolic tricks. In an effort not to be discovered, a demon may not answer some questions or give silly answers, unworthy of the intelligent spirit that he is. Other times he pretends to have left the body of the obsessed person by stopping all activity in hopes of removing the individual from the exorcist's care. Yet again, he will try every means to block an exorcism. He will manufacture physical or, more often, psychological obstacles to make the subject miss the appointment with the exorcist, unless a friend or relative forces the visit. At times he will manifest signs of a natural illness, most often psychological, to camouflage the symptoms of his presence. Sometimes the patient has dreams or visions in which he deludes himself that the Lord, Mary, or some other saint has liberated him. This way he avoids keeping his appointment with the exorcist, informing the priests that he has already been liberated.

The sacramentals that I mentioned, besides their specific individual use, can also mitigate the effects of the tricks that the evil one uses. When dealing with evil possession, tricks are the norm, and much prayer is needed to receive the grace of discernment. I will point out the following as the most frequent signs of evil influence: visions, locutions, false mysticism, or the claim to be a visionary. In these circumstances, when we are not in the presence of psychological illnesses, we are often confronted with the deception of demons.

I end this chapter with an anecdote concerning blessed water. Father Candido was exorcising a possessed individual. The sacristan approached him with the aspergillum and the bucket of holy water. Immediately the demon turned to him and said, "With that water you can wash your snout!" Only then the sacristan remembered that he had filled the bucket at the faucet but had forgotten to have it blessed.

Although the new *Book of Blessings*, which has been mandatory since April 11, 1993, changed the formulas, it has not diminished the effectiveness of these blessings, even if it does not explicitly cite all the benefits.

EXORCISING HOUSES

The Bible does not cite any exorcism of houses, but experience demonstrates that in certain instances this is necessary and fruitful. The *Ritual* as well does not mention this type of exorcism. It is true that, at the end of the exorcism of Leo XIII, we ask a blessing for the place where these prayers are recited, but the prayer itself is an invocation for God's protection over the Church against the evil spirits, with no mention of places.

I will immediately say that I have never experienced places that were infested by spirits as some novels or movies describe, such as an old and deserted castle. This is simply an effort to present what is spectacular and sensational, without any trace of serious research. In reality we often encounter noises such as squeaks or thumps. Many times there is a sensation of being watched by an invisible someone, or stared at, or touched, or assaulted. Fear plays a large part in these feelings, turning shadows into reality.

There are also many and more complex issues. Examples are doors and windows that open and close at a certain hour; steps walking down hallways; objects that move, or disappear to reappear in the unlikeliest places; and animals that are heard but cannot be seen.

I remember, for instance, that all the members of one family could hear the opening and closing of the front door and then the unmistakable sound of a man's steps crossing the hall, to disappear in some room. Once a friend who was visiting heard the same noises and asked who had come in.

To avoid scaring him, the family told him that it was an overnight guest. I am aware of insects, cats, and snakes that suddenly materialized. One individual whom I was exorcising even found a live toad in his pillow!

The presence of evil is manifested by physical discomfort; insomnia, headaches, or stomachaches; or a general malaise that happens in that particular place and nowhere else. When this happens it is easy to go to a doctor for a check-up, but it is not easy to isolate the causes. For instance, a person claims that every time he is the guest of a certain relative or friend he experiences the same discomfort, such as insomnia, headaches, or other pains that can last for days, while these symptoms are not present anywhere else. The diagnosis is easy, but not the cause of the problem, which can have many different origins. It could simply be the fruit of autosuggestion, if there are reasons to support it—for instance, a daughter-in-law visiting in-laws who were against the marriage or who are very possessive of their son. However, evil causes cannot be automatically excluded.

It is worth mentioning that the behavior of house pets when these phenomena occur is very interesting. For instance, if there is a feeling of an invisible presence in a room, a cat or a dog often fixes its eyes toward a particular spot. Other times, the animals will jump up and run away in terror, as though a mysterious presence advanced on them. I could mention many interesting details for those who are interested in researching this topic. Here I will simply say I believe that, while animals do not see anything concrete, they are much more sensitive to a strange presence than we are. I do not deny that the behavior of the house pets can be one of the deciding factors to determine whether to exorcise a house or not.

It is most important to question very carefully individuals who appear to be severely affected by this type of occurrence before proceeding with an exorcism. For the most part these phenomena are not due to an evil presence in a house, but in an individual. Many times I have had no success in exorcising a house, but when I went on to exorcise an individual or individuals, the phenomena in the house decreased and eventually disappeared.

How do we exorcise houses? Father Candido and I use the same method. The *Ritual* includes about ten prayers asking the Lord to protect places from evil influences. They include the blessing of homes, schools, and other buildings. We intone a few of these prayers. Then we read the first part of the first exorcism of individuals, modifying it to address a building. Next we exorcise every room, just as though it were a normal house blessing. Following this, we make another round, this time with blessed incense. We end with other prayers. After the exorcism, it is very efficacious to celebrate a Mass in the house.

If the disturbances are slight, one exorcism is sufficient. If the troubles are caused by a curse, and the curse is renewed, the exorcism must also be repeated until the house becomes "evil proof". In the worst scenario the difficulties are many. For example, I have found myself exorcising apartments that had been used for a long time to hold seances or where warlocks had practiced black magic. The worst examples involved satanic rituals. At times the gravity of the disturbances and the difficulty of total liberation were so great that I was forced to recommend simply leaving the place.

In other, less serious circumstances, prayer is sufficient to reestablish peace. One family was bothered by noises at night; after ten Masses were celebrated, the noises ceased completely. Could it have been poor suffering souls in purgatory who, by divine permission, were able to ask for intercession? It is hard to say, but it happened more than once. Father Pellegrino Ernetti, the most famous exorcist in the Venice area—who is also famous as a biblical and music scholar—experienced some very serious cases. One family was subjected not only to doors and windows that, although well secured, would open and close at will but also to flying chairs, dancing armoires, and other incredible events. The exorcist was finally successful by concurrently using all three sacramentals that are the standard tool of exorcists. He advised the family to mix in a cup or glass exorcised water, oil, and salt; then, every evening, to pour a teaspoon of the mixture on the ledge of every window and at the threshold of every door, praying the Our Father while doing it. This cure proved to be decisive. After a while the family stopped this practice, and in a matter of one week the disturbances started again, only to stop immediately when the exorcist's routine was reinstated.

I have also been asked about the possibility of infestation of house pets. Is it possible? What is the remedy? The Gospel tells us about that legion of demons who asked Jesus' permission to enter the herd of swine. Jesus allowed it, and the entire herd rushed into the Gerasene sea (Mt 8:28–33). I know of an inexperienced exorcist who ordered a demon to enter a farmer's family pig: the animal became savage and attacked the farmer's wife. Needless to say, the pig was immediately killed. These are rare instances, and every time they lead to the immediate death of the animal. I was told of a warlock who used his cat to deliver cursed items to their destination; here I would say that it was the master who was possessed and not the animal. It is often said that the cat is an animal who "absorbs spirits" and that evil spirits assume the semblance of a cat to go undetected. For certain warlocks and some forms of magic the use of cats is fundamental. I want to make it clear that it is not the fault of this charming house pet.

The infestation of animals is possible, and therefore so is the blessing of deliverance. In this, as in all other cases, the exorcist must discover the reasons behind the evil manifestation. The knowledge is necessary to avoid mistakes, although I will not address the matter in this book.

I will mention that since the first centuries of Christianity, we find instances of exorcisms performed on houses, animals, and things. Among others, Origen testifies to this practice. The *Catechism of the Catholic Church* rightly speaks of exorcism not only for persons but also for objects (1673).

THE CURSE

I have already mentioned that a curse can cause an innocent person to be attacked by demons. Since this is the
most common circumstance, I must discuss it separately. I
will try to use specific words. There is not a universally
accepted terminology; therefore every writer must define
his own terms.

Curse is a generic word. It is commonly defined as
"harming others through demonic intervention". This is
an exact definition, but it does not explain the cause of the
harm, hence the beginning of confusion. For instance,
some believe that *curse* is synonymous with *spell* or *witchcraft*. In my opinion, spells and witchcraft are two different
types of curses. I do not claim to give a comprehensive
explanation, and I rely solely on my own experience when
I define the following forms of curses. They are different
but not independent; crossovers are frequent: (1) black
magic, (2) curses, (3) evil eye, and (4) spells.

1. *Black magic, or witchcraft, or satanic rites that culminate with
black masses*. I will address these practices under one heading because of their analogy. I list them in order of gravity.
Their common characteristic is to obtain a curse against a
specific person through magic formulas or rituals—at times
very complex—by invoking the demon, but without the
use of particular objects. Whoever devotes himself to these
practices becomes a servant of Satan through his own fault.

Here I will discuss them only as instruments to harm others through curses.

Scripture very decisively forbids these practices because they are a rejection of God and a turning toward Satan: "There shall not be found among you any one who burns his son or his daughter as an offering, any one who practices divination, a soothsayer, or an augur, or a sorcerer, or a charmer, or a medium, or a wizard, or a necromancer. For whoever does these things is an abomination to the LORD" (Dt 18:10–12). "Do not turn to mediums or wizards; do not seek them out to be defiled by them: I am the LORD your God" (Lev 19:31). "A man or a woman who is a medium or a wizard shall be put to death; they shall be stoned with stones, their blood shall be upon them" (Lev 20:27), also Leviticus 19:26–31. Exodus is not more lenient: "You shall not permit a sorceress to live" (Ex 22:18). Other cultures also punished black magic with death; even if the terminology they use is different, their meaning is very clear. I will say more on this subject later on.

2. *Curses.* Curses invoke evil, and the origin of all evil is demonic. When curses are spoken with true perfidy, especially if there is a blood relationship between the one who casts them and the accursed, the outcome can be terrible. The most common instances that I have encountered involved parents or grandparents who called down evil upon children or grandchildren. The most serious consequences occur when the evil wish is against someone's life or when it is pronounced on a special occasion, such as a wedding. The authority and the bonds that tie parents to their children are stronger than any other person's.

I will give three typical examples of curses. I helped a young man whose father wished evil upon him at birth (he obviously did not want this child) and continued to do so as long as the son lived at home. This poor young man suffered from every conceivable misfortune: he had poor health, he could not find a job, his marriage was difficult, his children became ill. The exorcisms were able to help him spiritually, but nothing more. A second case involved a young woman who wanted to marry a worthy young man whom she loved very much. Her parents were opposed, but when all their efforts failed they went to the wedding. That same day the father took the daughter aside with an excuse and called down upon her every evil that he could think of against herself, her husband, and their future children. And it all happened despite exorcism and intense prayer.

One more example. Once a well-educated man came to see me. He rolled up his pants and showed me his legs, horribly scarred by a succession of surgeries, and told me his story. His father had been a very intelligent young man; his father's mother had wanted him to become a priest no matter what, but he did not think he had a vocation. Eventually life at home became unbearable, and the young man had to leave. He graduated from college, became successful in his profession, married, and had children. All this after a definitive break with his mother, who refused to see him for any reason. This man then showed me a photo of himself at the age of eight, taken by his father. It was the picture of a beautiful boy with a captivating smile, in short pants, bare knees, and the long socks that were in fashion at the time. His father had had the unhappy idea of sending this picture to the boy's grandmother, hoping that at the sight of this beautiful grandson she would agree to a reconciliation. Instead she sent this message: "May the legs of that child be always ill, and if you ever come back to this village you will die in the bed in which you were born." And so it happened. The man told me that his father went back to the village years after his mother's death, but he immediately felt ill; he was taken to the house in which he had been born, and he died the very same night.

3. *The evil eye.* This consists in a spell cast by looking at someone. It does not come about, as many think, by believing that some individuals cause bad luck by just looking at you; this is nonsense. The evil eye is a true spell; in other words, it presupposes the will to harm a predetermined person with the intervention of demons. In this instance the nefarious deed is achieved through the sense of sight. While I could never be certain that a particular spell was the result of the evil eye and whether a look had been sufficient, the effects were clear. Many times the perpetrator of the spell is not known, nor how it began. What is important is that the victim should not suspect everyone he meets but *forgive wholeheartedly whoever caused him evil*, no matter who. I want to stress that, while I believe that the evil eye is possible, I cannot be positive that I have encountered it in my experience as an exorcist.

4. *The spell (also known as malefice or hex).* This is by far the most commonly used means to achieve evil. The name (in Latin, *male factus*) means to do evil, that is, to make or manufacture some object with the most diverse and strange materials. This object has an almost symbolic value: it is a tangible sign of the will to harm, and it is offered to Satan to be imprinted with his evil powers. It is often said that Satan apes God; in this case we can use the sacraments as an analogy. The sacraments use tangible matter (for instance, the water of baptism) as an instrument of grace. In the malefice matter is used as an instrument of harm.

There are two distinct ways a hex is applied to the designated target. The *direct way* consists of mixing the object that is used for the spell into the victim's food or drink. As already mentioned, this is manufactured with the most diverse materials; it can be menstrual blood; bones of dead people; various burned powders, mostly black; animal parts—the heart seems to be the favorite; peculiar herbs; and so on. But the evil efficacy is not so much in the material used as in the will to harm through demonic intervention. This will is manifested in the black magic formulas that are chanted while mixing this material. Almost always the person who is struck by a hex, besides other symptoms, suffers a characteristic stomachache with which exorcists are very familiar and that is healed only after much vomiting or through the feces, and the strangest objects are expelled.

The second manner to apply a malefice is the *indirect way* (here I refer to the terminology that Father La Grua uses in his book *La preghiera di liberazione*. This consists in hexing objects that belong to the target (photographs, clothes, or other belongings) or figures that represent the accursed: dolls, puppets, animals, even real people of the same age and sex. This is called "transfer" material, and it is struck with the same ills that are intended for the victim. A doll is a very common example: during this satanic rite, pins are stuck all around a doll's head. As a result, the victim suffers from intense headaches and comes to the exorcist saying, "It is as though my head were crisscrossed by sharp pins." It may be that needles, nails, and knives are stuck in the doll's body as a "proxy" for the intended victim. Regularly, the accursed feels excruciating pain that wracks those very same points. Some people called "sensitive", of whom I will speak later, are able tell to the victim: "You have a hatpin crossing you from this to that point" and reveal the precise locations. I have seen individuals expel strange and very long pins made of a substance resembling plastic or very flexible wood from the part that was targeted and immediately be released from pain. Liberation commonly follows the expulsion of the most unusual materials: colored cotton thread, ribbons, nails, rolled-up wire.

A malefice that takes the form of "binding" deserves a special mention. Whichever material is used for the transfer of evil is tied to hair or colored cloth strips (especially white, black, blue, or red, according to the desired result). Once, for example, to strike the fetus of a pregnant woman, a doll was bound from neck to umbilical cord by means of a needle threaded with horsehair, with the intent of deforming the baby by causing an abnormal development of the organs included between the "bonds". This really happened; fortunately the harm proved to be less severe than intended. Bindings are specifically used to inhibit the development of certain body parts, but most often they are used to arrest mental development. Ties to the brain are inflicted to cause in the victims an inability to study, work, or exhibit normal behavior. When this malefice is successful, doctors are unable to identify the source of the illness and to cure it.

It also often happens that the proof of a hex shows up in pillows and mattresses in the form of strange objects. If I were to tell of the bizarre, unbelievable facts that I have witnessed, I could go on forever. I have found just about everything, from colored and tied ribbons to chunks of hair tightly knotted; knot-filled string and wool that was thickly braided by superhuman strength in the shape of crowns; animals—especially mice—or geometric shapes; and blood clots. I have seen chunks of wood or iron, twisted wire, and dolls full of piercing and marks and have witnessed the sudden appearance of very thick braids of children or women's hair. All these things are inexplicable without the intervention of an invisible hand. Sometimes these strange objects are not visible when the pillow or mattress is first opened, but after aspersion with exorcised water, or if a blessed image is put on them—especially a crucifix or an image of Mary—the most bizarre objects materialize. I will return to this subject in the following pages.

Now I believe is the time to repeat the advice that Father La Grua recommends in his previously mentioned book, *La preghiera di liberazione:* "Even though what I wrote is the result of direct experience, we must not believe too easily in curses, especially those cast through the means of malefice." Hexes are always rare. When the complaints that are brought to the exorcist are analyzed, they almost invariably reveal psychological causes such as suggestiveness and false fears. Also, curses are often unsuccessful for many reasons, for instance, because God does not allow the evil, or the intended victim is a person of deep prayer and union with God. Additionally, many sorcerers are inexperienced or unable to follow through; others are simply swindlers; or the devil himself, "liar from the beginning", as the Gospel brands him, fools his own servants. It would be a most grave error to live in fear of falling victim to a hex. The Bible never tells us to fear the devil; instead we are told to resist him in the certainty that he will flee from us (James 4:7) and to remain watchful against his attacks, by remaining firm in our faith (1 Pet 5:9).

We have been given the grace of Christ, who defeated Satan with his Cross; we have the intercession of Mary, who has been an enemy of Satan since the beginning of humanity; we have the help of the angels and the saints.

Most of all, at baptism we have been sealed with the Holy Trinity. If we live in communion with God, it is Satan and all of hell who tremble at our presence—unless we ourselves open the door to him.

Since the curse is the most common form of diabolical influence, I will add a few other insights, which I have gained through experience.

The curse may assume different characteristics, according to the end that is desired. For instance, it may be called "divisive" if it is intended to separate spouses, engaged couples, or friends. Many times I have dealt with engaged couples who loved each other, broke up without any apparent reason, and never managed to reconcile. I later found out that one of the couple's parents was against their marriage and turned to a practitioner of black magic to break the engagement. Another type of curse may be called "infatuation", which is used to lead someone to "fall in love". I know of a girl who fell in love with her best friend's fiancé. After fruitlessly trying to make him return her love, she went to a sorcerer. The engaged couple separated, and the man married the girl who commissioned the curse. Needless to say, it was a horrible marriage; the husband was unable to leave his wife, but he never loved her and always had the feeling that he had been forced to marry her.

Other curses are called "illness", because the target will always be sick. The so-called death curse is named "destruction". In this case, it is sufficient that the targeted individual invoke the protection of the Church: in other words, that the individual begin to pray, to ask others to pray intensely, and to seek exorcisms, and death will be avoided. I have followed many such cases; I have already mentioned that the Lord at times intervened miraculously, or at least in ways that are humanly inexplicable, to save the lives of these individuals from deadly dangers and, in particular, from suicide attempts. Almost always (I should say *always*, at least, in those instances of which I am aware) when the curse is powerful it also includes diabolical oppression, or even possession. That is why exorcism is necessary. The most dreadful curses can be those that are intended for the destruction of an entire family or to strike an entire family.

Norm number 8 of the *Ritual* for exorcisms cautions against referring those who are the target of curses to sorcerers or warlocks or other individuals who are not ministers of the Church. The use of any form of superstition or other illicit means in an attempt to be healed is forbidden. Experience teaches that this warning is necessary. Sorcerers are many; exorcists are rare. Unfortunately, some writers have advised going to a sorcerer for help against curses, even if the patient suspects that he will be the target of yet another curse. Such advice is an unpardonable mistake, especially coming from well-regarded and experienced authors, in books that are otherwise praiseworthy. This warning is especially important because the tendency to turn to sorcerers, warlocks, witch doctors, and such is as old as the world itself. Despite the social, cultural, and scientific progress, the habit of consulting the ministers of the occult seems to coexist peacefully with our "modern world". All social classes, even those most educated, are involved—engineers, doctors, teachers, politicians, and so on.

Norm number 20 of the *Ritual* suggests asking the demon the cause of his presence, particularly whether it is due to something the individual ate or drank. If this is the case, the exorcist must command the person to vomit. If instead the curse is due to some foreign object, the exorcist must ask to be shown where the object is hidden, find it, and burn it.

These are all useful suggestions. In fact, when food or drink is the vehicle through which a curse is delivered, we will always encounter that particular stomachache which I mentioned before; in this case, liberation always occurs through physiological means. The use of exorcised water, salt, or oil will greatly help the process. It is also possible that some cursed objects are expelled in mysterious ways, as I have already explained: for instance, the victim may suddenly feel a strange weight in the stomach, almost like a rock. After a while, he finds a rock on the ground, and the pain disappears. Other objects—colored strings, braided cords, and many other items—may be found. They must all be sprinkled with blessed water—the individual himself can do this—then burned in the open and the ashes thrown into running water. Items that cannot be burned, such as wire, must also be thrown into running water, either a river or the sewer. Nothing must be thrown into the toilet or sink; when this happens, often the entire house is flooded, or every drain becomes plugged.

Often the strange objects discovered in mattresses or pillows were not found by questioning the demon but through the indication of charismatic or sensory individuals—I will return to this subject—after which the exorcist is called. At this point it is also necessary to burn the mattress or the pillows outdoors, after sprinkling them with holy water, and to deal with the ashes as I mentioned above.

It is important that, while the cursed objects are burning, everyone pray. We cannot be too careful, especially when the curse is discovered by chance or through demonic revelation. During my training Father Candido told me of an error that he had made at the beginning of his career.

Father Candido and another Passionist priest, both authorized by the bishop, were exorcising a girl. While questioning the demon, they discovered that the girl was under a malefice. They asked for its form, and they were told that it was a wooden box, the size of a hand. They asked for the precise location and were told that it was buried three yards deep, near a certain tree. Full of zeal and armed with a spade and a hoe, they went digging on the spot. They found the box, just as they had been told, opened it, and found an obscene figurine among a lot of junk. They sprinkled everything with alcohol and immediately burned everything carefully, until only a pile of ashes remained. But they did not bless the objects before burning them, and they forgot to pray throughout the process, invoking the protection of the Blood of Christ. They had repeatedly touched those objects without immediately washing their hands with holy water. The end of the story is this: Father Candido was in bed for three months with a severe stomachache; these pains continued for ten years with less intensity, and they recurred periodically afterward. This was a tough lesson, but it was useful to me and to anyone who may be in the same situation.

I also asked Father Candido if, after all that suffering and hardship, the young woman was liberated. The answer was negative; she felt no benefit. This teaches us that, at times, hexes do all their damage when they are first put into place: finding the objects and destroying them later is useless. I dealt with several similar cases in which between the time of casting of the malefice and that of finding the objects many years had gone by. The hex had already accomplished all its evil work, and no benefits were felt when the object was found and destroyed. What helped, later on, were exorcisms, prayers, and the sacraments.

Under other circumstances burning the object stops the malefice; for example, the so-called hexes unto death by putrefaction. Once, while investigating a hex, I discovered that some cursed meat was buried. Fortunately it was found and destroyed before putrefaction, and thus the death of the accursed was avoided. Sometimes animals are buried alive, especially toads, leaving an air pocket around them to enable them to breathe for a while. If they are found before they die, the hex is broken. Nevertheless, the primary tools against the malefice are exorcism, prayer, the sacraments, and sacramentals.

I cannot overemphasize the importance of turning to God and his means of liberation instead of a sorcerer or a magician, even when we are under the impression that God's ways are slow. The Lord gave us the power of his name, the strength of prayer—both individual and in community, and the intercession of the Church. Turning to a sorcerer, to someone who hides his actions under the false name of "white magic" (which is always an appeal for Satan's help, as anyone who uses a curse to take away another curse does), can only aggravate the evil. The Gospel talks about a demon who leaves a soul to come back later with seven demons worse than himself (Mt 12:43–45). This is what happens when we turn to witchcraft. I will give three typical examples.

First example: someone begins to feel physical pain. He tries many doctors and medications, but the pain increases rather than diminishing; no cause can be found. At this point he goes to a sorcerer, or to a card reader who practices magic, and is told, "You are under a malefice. If you wish, I will remove it. I only ask for one thousand dollars." The patient thinks about it for a while, then pays the money. Sometimes he is asked for a photo, an item of intimate apparel, or a lock of hair. After a few days the man feels well and is convinced that he spent the money wisely. Thus, the demon left. After one year the same ailments begin to reappear. The poor victim starts his now-familiar journey from doctor to doctor, but medicine becomes more and more impotent, and the pain increases dramatically. When he cannot take it any more, the victim thinks, "That sorcerer asked me for one thousand dollars, but he took the pain away." At this point he goes back, without realizing that it was the sorcerer himself who caused the greater pain.

This time he is told, "Your spell is greater than the other one. I will take it away for only five thousand dollars; I would ask twice as much from anyone else." And thus the victim starts all over again; if he finally decides to turn to the exorcist, he must be liberated not only from the initial evil but also from the greater one caused by the sorcerer.

Second example; same as above. The patient pays, is healed by the sorcerer, and remains healed. However, his illness is transferred to his wife, children, parents, and siblings. In this case the evil is still multiplied. It can take the form of an obstinate atheism, a sinful life, a series of car accidents, misfortunes, depressions, etc.

Third example, same as numbers one and two: the patient is healed, and the healing remains. However, that evil was originally permitted by God for the expiation of the victim's sins, to encourage him to begin a life of prayer and sacramental grace and to return to the Church. The purpose of that illness was to obtain great spiritual fruits for the salvation of his soul. When the healing is achieved through demonic intervention, the conversion that the Lord desired to bring about through the illness does not come to pass.

We must keep clear in our minds the fact that God allows trials for our own good. He allows the cross only because it leads us to heaven. This truth is evident, for example, when people who have been given special charisms are struck by much pain. In these cases we must not pray for healing. Everyone remembers Padre Pio, who for fifty years bore the excruciating pain of the stigmata. Nobody dreamed of asking the Lord to remove the stigmata; it was all too clear that this was God's means to a great spiritual end. The demon is sly; he would have been all too glad to remove the marks of the Lord's Passion from Padre Pio's flesh! The opposite is true when it is the devil who causes the stigmata and brings forward false mystics.

MORE ON WITCHCRAFT

Witchcraft encompasses a vast range of topics. Volumes on the topic are so numerous that they would fill a library. It has been practiced throughout human history and by all civilizations. Still today many fall into its clutches. Many priests underestimate the danger of witchcraft. While they rightly trust in the salvific power of Jesus, who died to free us from Satan's bonds, they forget that the Lord never told us to underestimate the devil's power; he never told us to defy him or to stop fighting him. Instead God gave us the power to expel demons and talked of our endless struggle against him who "asks to sift us". Jesus himself underwent temptations by Satan and showed us clearly that we cannot serve two masters.

It is amazing how often the Bible warns against witchcraft and sorcerers, both in the Old and the New Testaments. Scripture warns us that witchcraft is one of the most common means used by the devil to bind men to himself and to dehumanize them. Directly or indirectly, witchcraft is a cult of Satan. Those who practice any sort of magic believe that they can manipulate superior powers, but in reality it is they who are manipulated.

Witch doctors believe that they own good and evil. Mediums and spiritualists invoke powerful spirits or the souls of the dead, without realizing that they have given themselves body and soul to demonic powers. Even if it is not immediately evident, these powerful spirits always use their minions for destructive purposes. When man is separated from God, he is poor and unhappy; he is unable to understand the meaning of life, and even less the meaning of hardships, suffering, and death. He longs for the happiness that the world holds out as a lure: wealth, power, health, love, pleasure, and admiration. It seems as though the devil is saying, "If you, then, will worship me, it shall all be yours" (Lk 4:6–7).

Thus we see everyone—young and old, women, laborers, professionals, politicians, and actors—seeking the "truth" about their future. This sort of crowd will always find another crowd: sorcerers, soothsayers, astrologers, card readers, prana therapists, and fortune-tellers of all kinds. Those who turn to them are motivated by chance, or hope, or desperation, or as an experiment. Some become victims, others remain bound, still others enter into the closed-end circle of sects.

What is behind all this? The ignorant believe it is only superstition, curiosity, fiction, fraud; in fact, it generates large sums of money. In reality, magic is not only a silly superstition, something without basis; it is also a recourse to demonic powers to influence the course of events or to manipulate others for personal profit. This deviant form of religiosity, which was typical among primitive peoples, has persisted throughout time and continues to coexist side by side with many religions in every country. Although its forms are many, the result is one: to distance man from God in order to lead him to sin and spiritual death.

There are two kinds of magic: imitative and contagious. *Imitative magic* is based on the concept of similarity in form and practice—it rests on the principle that everything generates something similar. A puppet represents the target, and, after the appropriate "ritual prayers", which are recited while piercing the body of the puppet with pins, the victim will also feel pierced and begin to suffer pain or illness in the same parts of the body that were pierced in the puppet. *Contagious magic* is based on the principle of physical contact, or contagion. To have influence over the target, the sorcerer must have access to something of his, such as hair, nail clippings, clothes. A photograph will do, better if it shows the entire body; the face must always be uncovered. In this type of magic, one part represents the whole. In other words, what is done to one part will have an effect on the entire person. Thus the sorcerer will use the appropriate rituals or formulas during preestablished times of the year and of the day. The evil work will come to fruition through the intervention of the spirits that he invokes. We have already talked about this when speaking about hexes, but witchcraft encompasses a much wider field than simple spells do, and greater still than the evil eye.

In one of the rites of initiation into black magic, the witch doctors of the island of Green Cape claim that, at one point during the ritual, the novice will find himself in front of a mirror through which Satan himself will appear to grant him "the powers" and to place in his hands the weapons that he will use. The weapons that the Christian has against the "roaring lion" are truth, justice, faith, and the double-edged sword of God's word. Instead, the witch doctor will have a real sword to wound men. He will have the power of destruction, malediction, foresight, bilocation, healing, and more, according to what he will be expected to accomplish to obstruct God's plans and to what he is able to offer Satan. Besides himself, he can offer his children and other more or less naïve individuals who turn to him for help. The victim of witchcraft will, at the very least, feel a great aversion for all that is sacred—prayer, churches, images. Instead his life will be filled with all sorts of unpredictable forms of evil.

Once the "sacrificial" offering is made, and once the requested items—no matter how insignificant—are given, even the person who hired the sorcerer will often be affected. The witch doctor brings this about by suggesting ceremonial rituals such as visiting seven churches, lighting candles in a specific manner, sprinkling special powder, or wearing prescribed objects. By these rituals the victims contract a more or less strong bond with the devil; the consequences for body and soul are always negative. Many times mothers bring their children to sorcerers who give them some items to wear—when the troubles begin, some come to seek my help. To the inexperienced eye these items look like junk, but, because of evil consequences, they prove to be true curses. If we venture on enemy territory, we fall into his power even if we act "in good faith", and only God's powerful hand can free us from the ties by which we allow ourselves to be bound.

The acts of so-called high magic can be classified as sacralization, consecration, blessings, destitutions, excommunications, and curses. The aim of all these actions is to transform objects and people into "sacred symbols"—naturally, consecrated to Satan. The magic material is "magnetized" at specific times; these are the objectives of magic astrology. Each sorcerer wears so-called pentacles and prepares them for others as well. The names derives from the Greek *panta-klea*. They are generally medals whose symbols are "energy catalysis". According to the sorcerer, these symbols possess a particular celestial power, and we must not confuse them with talismans. A talisman is something that is meant to represent some peculiarity of the individual whom they are supposed to protect. They are one of the greatest attractions for the unfortunate clients who feel struck by bad luck, misunderstandings, lack of love, or poverty, and who gladly pay the price, at times exorbitant, demanded for these "lucky charms" that are supposed to free them from all their problems. Instead, these individuals bring upon themselves such a negative energy that it will damage not only them but also their entire families. Incense is used abundantly in the preparation of all these objects, as in all sorts of magic activities. This incense is offered to Satan and is clearly meant as a counterpart to the liturgical incense we offer to God.

Other forms of magic teach sorcerers how to prepare potions and other concoctions that generate a sensation of diabolical oppression in those who will consume them mixed with their food or drink. The victim will find not only disgusting objects in his body but also the evil spirits who were invoked during their preparation. The notorious "love potion"—which can force a horrible relationship (also called "binding")—is nothing less than a display of satanic power.

The Bible speaks about the devil for the first time when he tempts our forefathers under the guise of a serpent. In mythology, the serpent is always associated with the personification of knowledge. In Egypt, it is the sorceress Isis who knows the secrets of rocks, plants, and animals. She knows illnesses and cures; therefore, she can reanimate the body of Osiris. The snake is always represented coiled on itself, with its tail in its mouth—a symbol of the eternal cycle of life. We can also recall the boa constrictor of the Inca emperors, or the sacred boa of the Indians.

In voodoo, the androgynous snake Danbhalah and Aida Wedo guides its followers with a surety and precision that gives stunning results at any hour of day and night. This snake claims to know all the secrets of the Creator Verb through the "magic language", whose power is increased by sacred music. This is Haitian magic, which together with the original African and the imported South American magic (particularly from Brazil) called "macumbe" has great evil power. I have already mentioned that the toughest curses I have ever exorcised came either from Brazil or Africa.

Modern civilization managed to meld, but not change, some customs. Therefore, science and magic, religion and ancient practices cohabit in our world. Even today, especially in rural areas of Italy, very religious people turn to sorcerers as a remedy against all sorts of ills, from sickness to the evil eye, to find a job or a husband alike. We are talking about good people "who always go to church". Just as some mothers still teach their children, in good faith, the gestures and the words required to remove the evil eye on the eve of Christmas; or who tie around the neck of their sons or daughters—along with chains holding crucifixes or sacred medals—hairs of badgers, teeth of wolves, or red horns. These are all objects that, even if they are not "charged" with negativity through magic rituals, have ties to Satan through the sin of superstition.

Magic is always tied to divination, that is, the attempt to know our future through crooked paths. We only have to think of the popular custom of card reading—asking tarot cards to predict our future—this is the most common means of divination used by sorcerers and fortune-tellers. It is believed that the origin of tarot cards goes back to the thirteenth century. It was introduced by gypsies, who condensed into this "game" of cards their power to predict the future. The basis for the game is an esoteric doctrine that claims to fix the relationship between man and the divine world. I am not going to expand on this topic. I merely want to point out that the naïve person, stunned by the precision with which his past has been revealed, comes out of the session either in despair or full of futile hopes. He often becomes suspicious of his family and friends, and most especially he will form a sort of addiction to the individual who read his cards that will endure into the future and cause feelings of fear, rage, and uncertainty. He will constantly desire to turn to magic practices or to buy some talismans to counter the enemy inside, to whom he himself opened the door and who now is causing sickness, misfortune, etc.

The worst magic of African origin is based on *witch-craft*—whose aim is to harm others through magic—and on *spiritualism*—which intends to contact the spirit of the dead or superior spirits. Spiritualism is practiced in every country and among all peoples. The medium is the intermediary between spirits and men, lending his energy (voice, gestures, writings, etc.) to the spirit who wants to reveal himself. It may happen that these spirits—who are always and only demons—will possess some of those who participate in the seance. The Church has always condemned seances and participation in them. We never learn anything useful by consulting Satan.

Is it truly impossible to evoke the dead? Is it always and only demons who appear in seances? We know well that the doubt in the mind of believers is caused by one single exception. The Bible tells us that, when Saul turned to a medium and ordered her: "Divine for me by a spirit, and bring up for me whomever I shall name to you" (1 Sam 28:8), Samuel, who had been dead only a short while, truly appeared. God allowed this exception, but we should note the medium's surprised scream and the even harsher reproof of Samuel: "Why have you disturbed me by bringing me up?" (1 Sam 28:15). The dead must be respected and not molested. Since this is the only occurrence in the entire Bible, I want to point to it as an exception. I fully agree with the writings of a Protestant exorcist and psychologist: "It is sheer selfishness and cruelty to try and cling to our departed, or to want to call them back among us. What they need is eternal liberation, and not to become hobbled again by the things and the people of this world" (Kenneth McAll, *Fino alle radici* [Ancora], p. 141).

Many are tricked through their lack of faith and their ignorance. Endorsing certain dances, chants, clothes, and animals that are used in different voodoo or macumbe rituals may seem interesting from an ethnic or folkloric viewpoint. Four candles at the four corners of a street or a triangle of candles, of which one points to the ground, may appear to be a game or a harmless superstition. It is time to open our eyes. I especially direct this invitation to priests: these are all attempts to evoke demon spirits that may or may not harm someone in the end, but whose ultimate goal is always to separate the victim from God, to lead him to sin, anguish, alienation, and despair.

I have been asked if it is possible to strike an entire community through magic. My answer must be yes; however, this topic would require a separate research all by itself, and therefore I will limit my comments to a few points. It is possible for the demon to use one person to strike even a very large group—these groups can even take over or influence one or more nations. In our own times, I believe that this was the case of men such as Karl Marx, Hitler, and Stalin. The atrocities perpetrated by the Nazis, the horrors of communism, the slaughters of Stalin, for example, reached diabolic proportions. Outside the political field, I do not hesitate in pointing to some music as a tool of Satan, as is the frenzy that some singers instigate in crowded places, often reaching peaks of extreme violence and destruction.

There are other instances of evil influence, easier to control and to heal—although collective possessions have always been hard to cure. Some of these involved entire classrooms, associations, religious communities, and more. The demon's ability to trick and introduce errors of the worst kind into entire groups is incredible. There are those who insist that it is easier to trick a crowd than a single individual. It is certain that the devil can strike very large groups; however, almost always it is clear that human assent is involved, the human sin of free acceptance of satanic actions. The motives of this acceptance are many: wealth, power, vice, and more.

The effect of Satan's influence on groups is one of the most destructive and powerful. This is why the popes, especially recent ones, insist on alerting us—for example, Paul VI's speech of November 15, 1972, and John Paul II's speech of August 20, 1986.

Satan is our worst enemy, and he will remain so until the end of time. Therefore he uses all his intellect and power in an attempt to thwart the plans of God, who wills the salvation of all. Our strength is the Cross of Christ, his blood, his wounds, and obedience to his words and to his institution, the Church.

WHO CAN EXPEL DEMONS?

I believe that I have made it sufficiently clear that Jesus gave the power to expel demons to all those who believe in him and act in his name. I am referring to private prayer, which we can collectively call "deliverance prayers".

Exorcists receive an additional, particular power. I am speaking of those priests who are specifically assigned by their bishop. Using the formulas and prayers suggested by the *Ritual*, these priests administer a sacramental that, unlike private prayer, involves the intercession of the Church.

Much faith, much prayer, and fasting are always needed: on the part of both those who intercede and those for whom we intercede. It would always be best if a group of people would gather to pray concurrently with, but separately from, an exorcism. All priests, even those who are not exorcists, have a particular power that derives from their ministerial ordination. This is not an honor to their person but a service for the spiritual need of the faithful; to liberate from evil influences is one of the things that is required of a priest. Everyone can use common means to obtain grace—such as prayers of deliverance—independently from, or even during, the exorcism itself: for instance, putting a crucifix, or a rosary, or some relics on the head of the victim. The relic of the Holy Cross is most effective, because it is by this Cross that Jesus defeated Satan's kingdom. The relics of saints who are our particular patrons are also efficacious, as often are even simple blessed holy cards, such as those depicting Saint

Michael the Archangel, of whom demons are particularly afraid.

I believe that I would disappoint the readers if I did not at least touch upon what is now a veritable army of *people claiming charisms, seers, sensitives, prana therapists, healers,* and even *gypsies.* It is a very large groups of individuals—all the more so because bishops and clergy, with a superficiality that ranges from incredulity all the way to ignorance, have abandoned this pastoral field that properly belongs to them. I will devote a chapter to this topic as well. In the meantime, I will comment on the above-mentioned individuals.

First I will speak of people who can—or who claim they can—bring about liberation, but who often simply aim at healing. It is difficult to make a clear distinction in this field. The devil is at the root of every illness, suffering, sin, death—they are all consequences of sin. But there are also ills that are directly provoked by the evil one. The Gospel mentions some such cases: the woman who was stooped for eighteen years (paralysis?) and a deaf-mute. In both instances, a satanic presence caused the sickness, and the Lord healed them by expelling the demons. The rule of thumb that I sketched before is very useful—if an illness has an evil origin, there is no drug that will cure it, while prayers and exorcisms will. It is true that in the case of a lengthy diabolical possession the victim becomes subject to psychological problems and may need adequate medical care even after liberation. Here I am merely touching upon an area that requires specific expertise, such as an exorcist usually does not have. An exorcist must be aware of mental illness only to the degree that he should recognize when a psychiatrist is needed; he is not required to know about mental illness as much as a psychiatrist does. By the same token, the exorcist must be aware of parapsychological phenomena, but he cannot be a substitute for an expert in the field. The exorcist's specific domain is supernatural. He must have exact knowledge of supernatural phenomena and the relative cures. This premise is necessary, because here we are dealing with matters that touch upon the supernatural, the paranormal, and the preternatural—or diabolical.

Charisms. The Holy Spirit, with divine freedom, gives his charisms however and to whomever he pleases. These are not given to the glory or benefit of the receiver but as a service to his brothers. Among these charisms is the power to liberate from evil spirits and to heal from illnesses. These gifts can be given to individuals and also to communities. They are not tied to personal holiness but to the free choice of God. Experience tells us, however, that God normally grants these gifts to righteous people of proven humility who pray frequently and live an exemplary Christian life— this does not mean absence of faults! Today, there is an inflation of those claiming charisms who attract crowds of suffering people. How do we discern those who are real from impostors? The discernment belongs to the Church, which is entitled to use any and all tools she considers necessary for this discernment.

I know of cases in which ecclesiastic authorities intervened to alert the faithful against charlatans and swindlers. I do not know of any who are officially recognized to have such charisms. This is a complex and difficult problem, which is compounded because charisms can suddenly stop. Since no living person is confirmed in a permanent state of grace, it is possible that one who has received a charism becomes unworthy. I would like to suggest four guidelines for determining the presence of true charisms. (1) The individual or the community lives the Gospel in a profound way. (2) The individual or the community performs the services absolutely free—not even accepting donations, as through these it is easy to become wealthy. (3) The practices used must be common means to obtain grace approved by the Church, avoiding unusual or superstitious actions. For instance, they must not use "magic" formulas but prayers, the Sign of the Cross and imposition of hands, and nothing that could offend modesty. They should avail themselves of water, incense, and relics and avoid anything that is extraneous to the normal ecclesiastical use. They should pray in the name of Jesus. (4) The fruits must be good. This is an evangelical rule that sums up all the other rules, "the tree is known by its fruit" (Mt 12:33).

Other characteristics that are typical of healings obtained through charisms are the following: they are effective for all sicknesses, even those of evil origin—that is, caused by demons. These healings are not based on human ability or power but on prayer spoken with faith, on the strength of the name of Jesus, on the intercession of Mary and the saints. One with a genuine charism does not lose his strength and does not need to "recharge" with a period of rest, as is the case with healers, diviners, etc.: he is not subject to physical reactions but is simply an active conduit for grace. Charismatic healings tend not to highlight the individual's gifts but to praise God and increase faith and prayer.

I want to stress briefly what the Second Vatican Council recommends, but what has not always been followed. Rationalism and naturalism took over this ground: extraordinary manifestations, miracles, the presence of saints, apparitions. These are all occurrences that have been greeted with diffidence rather than gratitude; with condemnation without investigation or, at the very least, as enormous headaches. The prayer of the first Christians:

"Grant to thy servants to speak thy word with all boldness, while thou stretchest out thy hand to heal, and signs and wonders are performed through the name of thy holy servant Jesus" (Acts 4:29–30) is not repeated in any church. It seems that these gifts today are simply a nuisance.

Vatican II affirms that the Holy Spirit "distributes special graces among the faithful of every rank. . . . These charismatic gifts, whether they be the most outstanding or the more simple and widely diffused, are to be received with thanksgiving and consolation. . . . Still, extraordinary gifts are not to be rashly sought after. . . . In any case, judgment as to their genuineness and proper use belongs to those who preside over the Church and to whose special competence it belongs, not indeed to extinguish the Spirit, but to test all things and hold fast to that which is good" (*Lumen Gentium*, no. 12). It is evident that these guidelines are just about universally ignored within the Church. Therefore, the Council affirms in vain that whoever receives the gifts of the Holy Spirit—even a lay person—has the right and the duty to exercise them, under the guidance and the discernment of the bishops. I am glad to be witnessing the blossoming of endeavors directed to helping bishops in their work of discernment: for example, the Charismatic Movement of Assisi. This is a wide-open field that must be pursued.

Seers and sensitives. I deal with these two categories at the same time, because they have substantially the same characteristics. The first *see*, the second *feel*; both express what they have experienced through contact with objects or individuals. Rather than expounding on this theme, which encompasses many areas, I will limit my comments to my specific area of expertise: the influence of these individuals in the realm of evil influences on people, things, and houses.

Many times seers and sensitives have contacted me; at times I have directly called them and asked them to be present in prayer during some exorcisms, to find out what they saw or felt. I was able to discern that their answers were given by the spirit of knowledge.

Some, as soon as they see or come in contact with a possessed individual, immediately detect the problem. At times they feel uncomfortable around these victims; other times they can see the evil that touches them and can describe it. It is sufficient to give them a photograph, a letter, or an object that belongs to a person who is suspected of being possessed for them to detect whether everything is normal, or whether there is an evil presence, or even if the person is dangerous because he carries out evil activities against others. Even simply by hearing someone's voice they can identify a problem. For instance, individuals who believe they may be the subject of evil influences will call a seer or a sensitive and receive the correct answer. Seers and sensitives are often asked to walk into houses that, because of strange occurrences, are thought to be infested, and they can sense whether evil is present or not. They are able to detect objects that have been hexed and that must be burned to remove the malefice. For instance, they can point to a pillow or a mattress, and when it is cut open, the strange objects I described before are found. However, they are not always right; their "feelings" must be checked out. They are also able to track the life of someone, pointing with surprising precision at which age the evil influence occurred, how and why it happened, and the symptoms that are associated with it. At times they are even able to point to the author of the evil influence.

One day, as I was ushering into the parlor a man who had asked me to be exorcised, I remembered that I was supposed to call a "sensitive". I rushed to the telephone, and he immediately said, "You are about to exorcise a man in his fifties. At the age of sixteen he was subjected to an evil spell, out of hatred against his father. They offered him a glass of evil wine to drink, and they hid one hex at the bottom of a well. From then on this young man began feeling unwell, and his sickness increased because every remedy proved to be futile. After a few years his father died, and he began immediately to feel better. However, his brain has been so damaged that he is unable to work. Try and bless him, but I am afraid that nothing will come of it, because this is an evil that took root a long time ago." Everything turned out exactly as he predicted. On other occasions, while I was exorcising someone in the presence of a "sensitive", I was told which parts of the body I should bless with the stole or anoint with oil, because they had been particularly affected; at the end of the exorcism, the victim would confirm that these were the areas that caused him the greatest pain.

I could go on with many more examples. I will say that the seers and sensitives I have chosen to consult—among the many that I have been offered as such—have all been very prayerful individuals, rich in goodness and charity, and especially very humble. If I had not discovered them by chance or because someone informed me of their talents, they would never have told me. What are these talents? Charisms? Paranormal abilities? I tend to believe that it is a paranormal gift that the person uses to serve others. I do not exclude that it can be a charism. I have never noticed in these people any sign of tiredness or loss of strength. I have witnessed a gradual strengthening of these gifts through their use; this leads me to believe that we are faced with paranormal talents. I will add that it is very difficult to find true seers or sensitives. On the other hand, there are a multitude of people who believe they have and are reputed to have these gifts. We need to be very careful.

Healers. I will only mention those healings that occur through the transmission of a particular form of energy, mainly through the imposition of hands. We are fully in the field of professor Emilio Servadio, who is an Italian expert on paranormal phenomena. Since I am not an expert, I will just say that healers have no effect whatsoever on illnesses caused by evil, just as human knowledge and doctors have no effect.

Prana therapy. In the last few years there has been an explosion of individuals who claim to have these gifts, as well as of healers. I do not intend to try and explain the theory of *prana* or of *bioplasma*. Official science is researching this phenomenon but has not sanctioned it yet. I report the conclusions that Father La Grua reached in his book *La preghiera di guarigione*: "If healings occur through an energy that the healer transfers to the sick person, either through a psychic charge or through a different store of energy, they have nothing to do with charismatic healings. Additionally, there may be the danger of evil infiltration. That is why we need extreme prudence." I have known some truly selfless prana therapists, people of faith, who make their gifts available as a service to others in a spirit of true charity. Unfortunately, they are extremely rare—"two for every thousand"—a renowned Venetian exorcist, Father Pellegrino Ernetti, told me, validating the caution with which we view prana therapy. It is by accurately discerning the fruits and methods that we recognize the tree.

Sorcerers. I have already given them ample space. I will mention again that healings can occur through demonic intervention, possibly under the guise of extraterrestrial beings or guiding souls. Jesus himself cautions us against "false Christs and false prophets" (Mt 24:24). A different army of healers, completely separated from demonic power, is the multitude of false sorcerers, simple charlatans, or swindlers. These cheat people by giving them talismans, ribbons, and pouches. I burned a simple sheet from a notebook on which was scribbled a lot of nonsense wrapped around a coil of string: this "talisman" cost $8,000! Another man who came to me for help paid twice as much for a small bag of junk that was supposed to free him from a lot of ills.

Gypsies. I must say a few words about gypsies because they are everywhere in Europe. Rather than repeating what I have already said about card readers and scoundrels, I will focus on a different aspect of this phenomenon, through an example. I exorcised a woman who was possessed by demons; she had been suffering with many ills for a while but did not suspect an evil cause. Once, after helping a young gypsy girl, she was told, "Lady, you are sick because they put a hex on you. Bring me a fresh egg." The woman gave it to her, and the gypsy put the egg on the lady's breast, recited a brief formula that sounded like a prayer in a strange language—*rom*?—and then opened the egg, from which came out a small snake. A few months later, the same woman helped another young gypsy girl, from another tribe. She was told almost the very same words: "Lady, you suffer because someone put a hex on you. You must let someone remove it. Bring me a fresh egg." This time, the woman came back with her husband. The young gypsy put the egg on the breast of the lady, recited a brief formula that sounded like a prayer, and then opened the egg. This time, a lock of hair came out.

A friend of mine, who is a doctor in Rome, was coming out of the basilica of Saint John Lateran—where there are always gypsies begging for money—when a young gypsy girl approached him, asking for money. He reached for his wallet to give her one dollar, but he did not have any, so he gave her ten dollars. The gypsy girl told him, "You have been very generous with me, so I also want to be good to you." She proceeded to tell him of some physical problems—the doctor knew those problems very well, but, like a typical doctor, he had ignored them. She also warned him that he was the target of a fraud and that he had to put a stop to it. It all turned out to be true.

How do we explain these occurrences? It is not easy. Some gypsies seem to have paranormal powers that they transmit from generation to generation. These are exceptions. Among gypsies, sorcery is widely practiced, as is every form of superstition. They have done so for centuries and continue to hand these powers down from mother to daughter—it is always the women who practice them.

As an aside: there is always one strong temptation for charismatics, sensitives, and exorcists (for us even more than the others): the temptation of finding the quickest way to heal, by going outside the common sacred means to obtain grace and unwittingly falling into the trap of magic. We begin to see, for example, that if we use a small dish full of water, add a few drops of oil, and utter a few names we obtain some answers, and so we begin a series of magic practices. I have witnessed the lapse into magic practices on the part of some who fortunately recognized their error and were able to turn back onto the right path. Unfortunately, not everyone is able to do so. I have also known of priests—not exorcists—who used some methods of healing with some success, without realizing that they were turning to magic. The devil is shrewd: he is always ready to promise us the kingdom of this world, if we fall on our knees and adore him!

THE "CINDERELLA" OF THE RITUAL

Many years have gone by since the end of the Second Vatican Council. All the sections of the *Ritual* have been revised according to the Council's guidelines. There is only one section that is still sealed with the sign "Work in progress", the section that concerns exorcisms. It is true that we have the doctrine of Sacred Scripture, theology, and the Magisterium of the Church. I have detailed elsewhere some texts of Vatican II. I am not going to repeat the three speeches of Pope Paul VI and the eighteen of Pope John Paul II on the subject. I will limit myself to one sentence from the speech that Paul VI gave on November 15, 1972: "Whoever refuses to recognize the existence of [the demonic reality] denies biblical and ecclesiastic teachings. So does anyone who claims that this reality has its own beginning and that it does not originate from God, as every creature does, and anyone who tries to explain it as pseudo-reality, as a conceptual and fantastic personification of all unknown causes of our ills." Later on he adds: "The chapter on the demons, and on the influence that they can exert on single individuals, on communities, on entire societies, or on events, is a very important one for Catholic doctrine. We need to revisit it and study it; unfortunately, today it is practically ignored."

Today, for many ecclesiastics, these words of the Bible, of tradition, and of the Magisterium on the subject are wasted. Monsignor Balducci rightly writes, "It is well that the public knows what kind of crisis the Church is facing today, at least doctrinally!" (*Il diavolo* [Piemme], p. 163). I have been told that many of my writings are argumentative toward certain theologians, bishops, and exorcists. It is not a matter of being argumentative but of bringing the truth to light. This crisis is not only doctrinal; it is pastoral above all. That is, it involves bishops who are not appointing exorcists and priests who do not believe in this office anymore. I do not mean to generalize, but today the devil is most actively tormenting people, and when his victims look for an exorcist, they come up against the usual sign: "Work in progress".

I will start with theologians. I cite Luigi Sartori, who is one of the most well-known and quoted. He writes, "It is probable that some of Jesus' healings involved individuals affected by nervous disorders rather than by true demonic possession." This is an insinuation of the worst kind, and it is false. The Gospel always distinguishes between healings of people with diseases and liberations from demons, just as it clearly differentiates between the power that Jesus grants to heal illnesses and the one that he grants to expel demons. The evangelists may not be able to refer to the modern technical name of some disease, but they are fully capable of discerning when they are confronted by an illness and when by demonic possession instead. It is Luigi Sartori and not the evangelists who cannot distinguish between the two. We have stressed the fundamental importance that the expulsion of demons holds in Christ's activity. When the seventy-two disciples wanted to sum up the results of their ministry, after Jesus sent them out preaching two by two, they joyfully mentioned one thing, and one thing only: "Lord, even the demons are subject to us in your name!" And Jesus replied, "I saw Satan fall like lightning from heaven" (Lk 10:1–18). We should not be surprised that Luigi

Sartori concludes his article with this affirmation: "Jesus the miracle worker expressed above all the strength of love; he built relationships of mutual empathy; that is why he could work miracles, and not because he possessed sacred and secret powers, like a sorcerer" (*Famiglia Cristiana*, no. 19, May 10, 1989). No, dear theologian, Jesus was not looking for empathy and did not possess the secret powers of a sorcerer. He possessed the omnipotence of God, and with his actions he demonstrated that he was God. These "subtleties" seem to escape some modern theologians.

Take another theologian, Luigi Lorenzetti. He magnanimously admits that "the believer cannot exclude in absolute that there is a demonic explanation for certain occurrences"; but then he immediately adds, "It is difficult, rather, impossible to assert with certainty when such a presence occurs in concrete instances." If this is impossible, then neither the liberations affected by Christ nor those achieved by the apostles are to be believed. It follows that the power to expel demons that Jesus gave his Church is also useless and that the ecclesiastic norms that guide exorcisms are useless, and so are exorcists. No, dear theologian, it is impossible for you and theologians like you to determine the concrete instances of demonic presence because you have absolutely no experience in this field. Therefore, it is very convenient to conclude, "In general, we do not err if we substitute a scientific-natural interpretation to the magic-demonic one" (*Famiglia Cristiana*, no. 39, October 5, 1988). This is like saying I believe in demons in theory, because I do not want to be accused of heresy, but at the practical level I do not believe, because at the practical level I trust only natural science.

If this is how prestigious theologians think, what can simple priests believe? I touch with my own hands every day the results of this disbelief. At times these theologians put in the same basket exorcisms and the elaborate frauds perpetrated on the credulous public by those who want to make quick and easy money. I cite the example of a pastor in Palermo, Sicily, Father Salvatore Caione, who was quoted in *Famiglia Cristiana* (no. 6, February 8, 1989). With the heading "Hexes do not exist", he judges everything to be trickery and puts everyone at the same level: hex makers, card readers, and exorcists—it does not matter that these last are appointed by bishops in accordance with Canon Law. The fact that so many allow themselves to be duped is undoubted; however, it is not through errors that we teach the truth. These are subtleties that escape Father Salvatore and those who publish his opinions without noticing the monumental errors that they contain.

When we mix error with truth, we should not be surprised at the results. Exorcists are few and, therefore people turn to the swelling ranks of sorcerers. The believer is not taught by anyone. I exorcised a nun who was in pitiful condition as a result of a demonic possession that for ten years had steadily weakened her. I called her general superior and told her that she should not have waited until the sick person was near death before calling the doctor; she should have called him at the onset of the disease. The superior answered, "You are right, but these things have not been taught to us by any priest." She also told me how many priests—not to mention doctors—had seen that nun, and not a single one suggested that the true cause of a disease that was defying every known cure could have demonic origins.

It is true that in my writings I have also taken exorcists to task. I said that "we lost the school", meaning that in a diocese there is no longer that succession by which the experienced exorcist trained his replacement. Thus it happens that some exorcists are unaware of the most elementary procedures. I chided Monsignor Giuseppe Ruta, canon of the cathedral and coordinator of the exorcists in Turin, Italy. Franca Zambonini interviewed him on behalf of *Famiglia Cristiana* (March 30, 1988), as suggested by Cardinal Ballestrero. Ruta affirmed that "diabolical possession is limited in time and lasts only a few hours or a few days." This naïve answer reveals a total lack of the most elementary experience. In fact, he continues by saying that every person who turned to him "never exhibited any of the signs that require an exorcism". I myself, in nine years of exhausting work (so much so that I have been forced to cut back my workload), have exorcised over thirty thousand people, and I have noted the name of everyone who was possessed: ninety-three so far, and they had all been possessed for approximately ten years. There are people who undergo exorcisms at regular intervals over periods of ten, fifteen years or more, and they are still not liberated.

I have also strongly criticized Monsignor Giuseppe Vignini, who is the penitentiary of the cathedral of Florence, for the four articles that he published in *Toscana oggi* (October and November 1988). When an exorcist writes that magic, black masses, spell casting, etc., are nothing but "innocuous artificial practices, which stem from imaginative suggestions"; when he affirms that exorcism is not a sacrament but a simple invocation, ignoring that it *is* a sacramental; when he concludes his random thoughts with the statement that, in practice, exorcisms should never be performed, then I must tell him, with every due respect, "Dear son, either you learn your trade, or you change your job."

I know of some exorcists who do not even own a *Ritual* book; they are unaware of the norms that they must follow as well as of the prayers that they must recite. They know only the translation—and not intact—in Italian of Pope Leo XIII's exorcism and simply recite it. The world press reported with much publicity the case of Annelise Michel, of Klingenberg, Germany. She was a twenty-four-year-old girl who died in the summer of 1986 following a long series of exorcisms. The item made news because the two exorcists were accused and underwent legal trial. The data that was published in newspapers and other publications (such as the book by [Walter] Kasper and Lehmann, *Diavoli demoni possessione* [Queriniana, 1983]) hinted that the two priests involved were all too eager to suspect the presence of diabolic possession. It also appeared as though the exorcists—although they always acted with the consent and in the presence of the girl's parents—had allowed themselves to be led by what the girl herself told them would be useful for the liberation.

However, a later book researched the facts of the case in greater depth: *Annelise Michel*, by Kasper Bullinger (Altotting: Ruhland, 1983). This book studied the case and ended by substantially exonerating the two exorcists. It demonstrated that both the bishop who had authorized the exorcisms and the two priests had acted with the utmost propriety. The book also indicated the cause of the girl's death, which was completely independent from the administration and reception of the sacramental. In any case, this event contributed to the reluctance of priests to accept appointments as exorcists.

Finally, I come to the bishops. It is true that I have been upset with them, because I love them and wish for their salvation. The Code of Canon Law does not address the fault of "omission in office"; but the Gospel passage about general judgment, as reported by Matthew 25, gives us a clear indication that the sin of omission can be an unpardonable offense.

Still vivid in my mind is the most unfortunate statement by a famous archbishop on November 25, 1988, while he was a guest on a very popular television program hosted by Mr. Zavoli. This archbishop appeared to brag that he had never performed an exorcism and never appointed an exorcist. Fortunately, the honorable Formigoni, who is a member of the movement *Comunione e Liberazione*, was also on the program, and he presented the Christian viewpoint. Then I noted an entire series of comments by bishops who, without trying to generalize, are not a credit to the Italian episcopate. Such sentences were reported to me by persons from all over Italy, after I referred them to their bishops before I would grant them an appointment. I will mention the most common comments: "I do not appoint exorcists as a matter of principle." "I believe only in psychology." "Do you still believe in such things?" "I have not found any priest who is willing to accept this task. Go look elsewhere." "I do not appoint exorcists and do not practice exorcisms because I am afraid. If the devil becomes my enemy, what am I to do?" "I would like to know who put these idiocies into your mind." I could go on. Each one of these answers brought great suffering to the person who received it; I wonder if it reveals the same suffering by the person who gave it. The majority of these individuals contacted the bishop after they had been exorcised by Father Candido and had been warned by him that they needed additional exorcisms. That is, the victims approached their bishops armed with the diagnosis of a very famous and competent exorcist.

I do not mean to generalize. If I am an exorcist, I owe it to the sensitivity and initiative of Cardinal Poletti. I believe that every exorcist will witness on behalf of his bishop with the same gratitude. However, the scarcity of exorcists clearly denotes a lack of interest on the part of the episcopate in general.

If I mention other European nations, the picture is even worse than it is in Italy. I have exorcised people from Germany, Austria, France, Switzerland, England, and Spain. All these individuals came because of Father Candido's fame and in the end had to be satisfied with his student (myself). These individuals all testified that they had been unable to find an exorcist in their own country. A Swiss professional assured me that he had called every Catholic bishop in that country and received nothing but negative answers. I do not mean to say that there are no exorcists in these countries, but it is very difficult to find them. Coming to Rome specifically for an exorcism is not fun.

I reiterate my statement: the conditions abroad are worse than in Italy. I will give a significant example. My co-religious in the United States (the Society of Saint Paul) wanted to translate into English the book *Il diavolo*, by Balducci. They were finally able to obtain an Imprimatur after they agreed to remove all references to diabolic possession, at the specific request of the diocesan censor. This is the usual mistake: we do not deny the presence of demons in theory, because we do not want to look like heretics, but we will decisively deny it when we are faced with concrete examples.

On the other hand, some Protestant denominations do not take this approach. Even in Rome there are some who take the matter very seriously. They investigate an occurrence, and when after their process of discernment they find evidence of diabolical activity, they exorcise with an efficacy that many times I was able to witness personally. It

is obvious that not only Catholics but everyone who believes in Christ has the power to expel demons in his name.
We must not be jealous of anyone else, but should look to
the Gospel for guidance. When John told Jesus, "We saw a
man casting out demons in your name, and we forbade him
because he was not following us", the Lord rebuked the
apostles (Mk 9:38–40). This is what the members of the
renewal movement discovered when they set out on the
road of "Prayers of Deliverance". These prayers must be
guided by precise rules, but they are extremely efficacious.
Cardinal Suenens wrote a book specifically to regulate such
prayers, *Renewal and the Power of Darkness* (Pauline Editions,
1982), with a foreword by Cardinal Ratzinger. He writes,
"At the beginning, many Catholics tied to the renewal
movement discovered the practice of deliverance among
Christians of other traditions, belonging mainly to the Free
Churches or Pentecostals. The books that they read, and
still read, for the most part come from these denominations. Among their literature there is an enormous wealth
of information on the devil and his acolytes, on witchcraft
and its methodology, and so forth. In the Catholic Church,
this field has been left almost fallow. Our directives for
specific pastoral response are inadequate for our times" (pp.
79–80).

This is a complaint that I will address in my next chapter; here, I want to stress that it is right to learn from those
who better follow the Gospel recommendations. In this
respect, as in the study and dissemination of the Bible,
Catholics are lagging behind some Protestant denominations. I will never tire of repeating this: rationalism and
materialism have polluted a segment of theologians, and
their influence on both bishops and priests has been profound. It is the people of God who pay for these errors. I

know of only one bishop who is also an exorcist in Italy, the African Milingo, and he is opposed by every side. I know that Pope John Paul II has performed at least two exorcisms. I would be happy if anyone would provide me with additional information.

I openly admit that one of the purposes of my book is to contribute to the reestablishment of the pastoral practice of exorcisms in the Catholic Church. This is a precise mandate of our Lord, and the fact that it is not pursued is an unforgivable omission.

Appendices

Saint Irenaeus' Thought

I report the thought of one of the more ancient theologians, Saint Irenaeus, in order that some of our modern theologians may learn from it. I transcribe it from the monthly magazine Il segno soprannaturale, *September 1989, as edited by a great teacher under the pseudonym of ALPE.*

Irenaeus was born sometime around A.D. 140 in Asia Minor. He was bishop of Lyons and founded the Gallic Church. He died around A.D. 202, possibly as a martyr. His fundamental work is *Adversus haereses* (Against the heretics), in which he completely rejects the theses of the heretical sect of the gnostics. The gnostics claimed that the world was generated by an evil creator. Irenaeus rebuts that the true creator is the Logos—that is, the Word of the good God. The angels are a part of the cosmos that God created. The devil, like all other angels, was also created good; nevertheless, he was inherently and eternally a creature and as such was inferior and subordinate to God. The devil apostatized and therefore fell from heaven. That is why Satan is the *archetypal apostate*, and also the *imposter* of the universe, who "wants to trick our minds, darken our hearts, and try to persuade us to adore himself rather than God". His powers are limited because he is only the *usurper of that authority* which legitimately and fundamentally belongs only to God, and "he cannot force us to sin."

Satan, Irenaeus continues, lost his angelic grace because he was envious of God, "wishing to be adored himself". He is also envious of man, because man is the image and likeness of God. His envy is focused primarily against us. This is why he entered the Garden of Eden with his heart corrupted by the desire to bring our forefathers to ruin. Irenaeus is also the first Christian theologian to elaborate—and consequently develop—a theory of original sin. God created Adam and Eve and put them in paradise to live happily, in close relationship with him. Satan, knowing their weakness, entered the garden and tempted them under the disguise of a serpent.

Satan's wickedness might have been without any effect had not God given mankind the freedom to choose between good and evil. Satan "did not force" the first man and the first woman to sin; "they chose it freely, because God specifically created them with the greatest gift of freedom of choice. Satan is the only tempter, but also the true and tenacious one, because he is envious of the original state of our forefathers."

Through Adam and Eve's choice, all humans participated in their sin, and from that instant we made ourselves slaves of the devil. Worse, we are powerless to free ourselves from him by our own choice. Subjected to Satan, we have distorted the divine image and likeness that we possessed and have condemned ourselves to die. Eden's happiness was shattered. Since we turned our backs on God of our own free will, we placed ourselves in Satan's hands. It is therefore just that Satan held us in his power until we were redeemed. "Strictly speaking, from a viewpoint of justice, God could have left us in Satan's hands forever. However, in his mercy, he sent us his Son to save us." The salvific action of Christ begins with Satan's temptation of the second Adam (Jesus), as a "recapitulation" of the temptation of the first Adam. This time, the devil fails and is definitively defeated by Christ. Christian tradition gives us three main interpretations of the salvific action of Christ's Passion.

1. The first interpretation: human nature was sanctified, exalted, transformed, and saved by Christ's becoming a man.
2. The second interpretation: Christ was a sacrifice offered to God to reconcile him with man.
3. The third interpretation: the *theory of the ransom.* Irenaeus was the first strong supporter of this theory, based on the following assumptions: "Since Satan legitimately held the human race captive, God offered to ransom our freedom at the cost of himself. Only he could pay the price. Only God could freely subject himself; nobody else could freely choose, because our original sin had deprived us of all freedom. God the Father delivered up his Son, Jesus, to free us, who were hostages of the devil. The sufferings of Christ paralyzed the devil, liberating us from death and damnation."

The *theory of sacrifice*, which was the principal alternative theory during Irenaeus' time, claimed that Christ, at the same time man and God, assumed on himself all the sins of mankind and of his own free will delivered himself up to death, thus paying to God an adequate price. The *theory of ransom*, although at times it was poorly expressed, reflected the emphasis that the Fathers of the Church placed on the *cosmic battle* between Christ and Satan. This theory generally corresponded rather well with the moderate dualistic assumptions of early Christianity. According to Irenaeus, Christ is the second Adam, he who freed us from the chains of death that bound us as a result of the weakness of the first Adam. The notion of *recapitulation* (Christ the second Adam voids the damage caused by the first man) was at the core of Irenaeus' Christology: "Satan, defeated by Christ, continues to hinder our salvation with all of his energy. He encourages paganism, idolatry, witchcraft, wickedness, and especially heresy and apostasy. Heretics and schismatics who do not follow the true Church of Christ are members of Satan's legions. They are his agents in the cosmic war against Christ."

Irenaeus claims that the defense of Christians against the devil is Christ. The devil flees when Christians recite their prayers and when the name of Christ is spoken. Nevertheless, the battle is not ended yet, because the demons will continue to test all baptized, with the Creator's permission. This permission is granted "to punish them for their sins, in order better to purify them, and to teach them brotherly charity" of mutual aid in spiritual need with reciprocal comfort and endurance; but most of all, to keep them "always vigilant and strong in the faith".

A Vatican Document on Demonology

You must not think that I am the only one who has noticed the gross errors of certain theologians. It appears that many of those theologians adopted Rudolf Bultmann as a new father of the Church. Bultmann, among others, wrote, "We cannot use electric light and radio, or turn to modern medicine in case of sickness, and at the same time believe in a spirit world and in the miracles that the New Testament presents us" (*Nuovo Testamento e Mitologia* [Queriniana, 1969], p. 100). Assuming that technologic progress is proof evident that the word of God is outdated indicates an inability to think. Many biblical students and theologians believe that they are not "with the times" if they do not follow those directives. In the above-mentioned book, Lehmann cites an interesting statistic about Catholic theologians: two-thirds of them accept the traditional teachings on demons—in theory—but they reject these teachings at the practical, pastoral level. That is, they do not want to oppose the Church formally, but practically they do not accept her teachings (p. 115). Also interesting is another statistical datum: Catholic theologians demonstrated a very superficial knowledge of diabolical possession and exorcisms (p. 27). This has been my claim all along.

The Congregation for the Doctrine of the Faith is very aware of this condition and commissioned a study from an expert on the matter. The results were published in the Italian edition of *Osservatore Romano*, June 26, 1985, with the title *"Fede cristiana e demonologia"* (Christian faith and demonology). This article then became part of the official documents of the Holy See (*Enchiridion Vaticanum*, vol. 5, no. 38). I will cite parts of it. The main purpose is to educate the faithful, and even more those theologians who are misguided, who avoid mentioning Satan's existence in their studies and teachings, although "The reason the Son of God appeared was to destroy the works of the devil" (1 Jn 3:8). By taking away the existence of the devil, we destroy redemption; he who does not believe in demons does not believe in the Gospel.

> Throughout the centuries, the Church has always chastised various forms of superstition, excessive preoccupation with Satan and demons, different forms of cult, and obsessive attachment to these spirits. It would therefore be unjust to affirm that Christianity, forgetful of the universal lordship of

Christ, made Satan the preferred argument of her preaching, transforming the Good News of the resurrected Lord into a message of terror. . . . In reality, however, it would be a deadly mistake to behave as though we believed that history is already resolved, redemption has already achieved its full goals, and it is no longer necessary to participate in the fight that is spoken of in the New Testament and by teachers of spirituality.

More often, however, the existence [of Satan] is openly revoked by doubts. Some critics, believing that they can identify their position with that of Christ, contend that he never spoke words that guarantee the existence of the demonic world. They explain that any affirmation of Satan's existence simply reflects the ideas of Judaic writings, or it is merely a New Testament tradition and not Christ's affirmation. Therefore, since this tradition is not part of the central Gospel message, it should not strain our faith, and we are free to abandon it.

Other theologians, more objective and more radical, accept the statements of Sacred Scripture on demons as far as their obvious meaning. However, they hasten to add that, in today's world, these statements would not be acceptable even for Christians; they too, therefore, eliminate them. Finally, some believe that the idea of Satan, no matter what its source, is no longer relevant, and if we insist on justifying it, our teaching would lose credibility and would overshadow our focus on God, who is the only One deserving of attention.

Finally, all of the above claim that the name of Satan and devil are nothing other than mythical and functional personifications, whose purpose is only to underline dramatically the influence of evil and sin on humanity. Therefore, it is simply a manner of speech, and our modern times need to reinterpret it in order to find a different way to teach Christians the duty to fight against all the evil forces in the world.

These positions are presented with a great show of erudition by magazines and some theological dictionaries. It should cause great concern. The faithful are used to taking seriously Christ's warnings and the writings of the apostles.

Those who know biblical science cannot fail to realize that they are faced with a campaign to change public opinion and will wonder where this process of demythologizing, which started in the name of hermeneutics, will lead them.

The main healings of the possessed achieved by Christ took place on occasions that later proved to be decisive in the narration of his ministry. His exorcisms presented and directed the problem of his mission and his Person, as evident from the reactions that these exorcisms provoked. Jesus never placed Satan at the center of his Gospel, but spoke about him with important declarations at crucial moments.

First of all, he began his public ministry by accepting to be tempted by the devil in the desert. Mark's sober narration of this event is as decisive as Matthew's and Luke's description. Jesus then warned us against this adversary in his Sermon on the Mount and in the prayer that he taught his own, the Our Father; on these points, many biblical scholars—backed by liturgical practices—agree. The book of Revelation most of all is the grandiose fresco through which shines the power of the resurrected Christ according to the witness of his Gospel. Revelation proclaims the triumph of the slain Lamb, but we would fool ourselves completely on the nature of this victory if we did not see in it the end of a long struggle. A struggle that includes Satan, his angels, and their historical agents, both individually and through the intervention of human powers opposing the Lord Jesus. In fact, it is Revelation that finally unmasks Satan's identity by unveiling the enigmas of his many names and symbols throughout Sacred Scripture. The devil's action takes place throughout the centuries of human history, under the eyes of God. It is obvious that the majority of the Fathers, beginning with Origen, abandoned the idea that the fallen angels committed a carnal sin and saw that the beginning of their fall was in their pride—that is, in their desire to be elevated above their station, to affirm their independence, and to be thought of as gods. Next to pride, many Fathers underlined Satan's wickedness against man. According to Saint Irenaeus, the devil's apostasy began when he became jealous of man's creation and tried to make him rebel against his Maker.

Tertullian says that Satan attempted to counter God's plan of salvation by plagiarizing the sacraments instituted by Christ with magic mysteries. Therefore, patristic teachings faithfully and substantially echo the faith and the orientation of the New Testament.

PASTORAL DIRECTIVES TO BE REBUILT

"In my name they will cast out demons" (Mk 16:17). This simple affirmation that concludes the Gospel of Mark has been sufficient to serve as a complete pastoral directive for liberation during the first centuries of Christianity. Justin, Tertullian, and Origen tell us that every Christian was an exorcist, that is, had the power to expel demons, which was founded on faith and the name of Jesus. Then the formulas for exorcisms began to multiply and to be organized. In the meantime, the ecclesiastic authorities started to regulate exorcisms, entrusting the most severe cases solely to the care of competent individuals. At the same time the Church multiplied the sacramentals, allowing everyone to use them for lesser incidents.

Beginning with the seventeenth century, when the most serious exorcisms were reserved for bishops or for priests whom they delegated, as is the case today, every diocese enjoyed a sufficient number of exorcists. The current crisis of practical incredulity causes bishops to avoid facing a problem that should be part of every ordinary pastoral practice of every diocese—that of an adequate number of exorcists. Consequently, priests are neither prepared nor willing to accept the office. Canon Law exhorts parish priests in particular to be especially near families and individuals who are suffering; to assist the poor, the sick, the needy, and those who are undergoing severe trials (canon 529). There is no doubt that these directives include the specific needs of those who are victims of the evil one. But who believes these victims?

As a result, recourse to sorcerers, warlocks, card readers, and hex makers is escalating; there are very few victims who turn to an exorcist before they have suffered at the hands of those others. We are witnessing the fulfillment of the words of Sacred Scripture concerning King Ahaziah. While he was gravely ill, he sent messengers to consult Baalzebub (prince of demons!), god of Ekron, to find out his future. The prophet Elijah intercepted these messengers and asked them, "Is it because there is no God in Israel that you are going to inquire of Baalzebub?" (2 Kings 1:1–4). Today, the Catholic Church has abdicated this specific mission, and her children do not turn to God anymore, but to Satan.

"What are the greatest needs of the Church today? Do not think that our answer is simplistic or superstitious and unreal: one of the greatest needs today is the defense from that evil that we call the devil" (Paul VI, November 15, 1972). While the Pope's words are addressed to a much wider field, it is obvious that exorcisms are also included.

The committee that is working on the revision of the *Ritual* faces a very complex number of tasks. In addition to the revision of prayers and norms for exorcisms, it must also address the entire pastoral approach on the matter.

Currently, the *Ritual* directly mentions only demonic possession, which is the most severe and rarest of all demonic activity. In practice, exorcists take care of every type of satanic intervention: demonic oppression (much more numerous than full possession), obsession, infestation of houses, and other activity that appears to benefit from our prayers. The old saying that *"natura non facit saltus"* (nature does not jump, but goes forward slowly, through evolution) is also valid for satanic activity. For instance, there is no clear distinction between the oppressed and the possessed, just as the line between oppressed and other evils is not clear. Some physical illness can be caused by the evil one, just as he has undoubted influence in some forms of moral sickness (habitual state of grave sin, especially in its most severe instances). I have seen the benefits of practicing a short exorcism, besides the normal prayer for the sick, when I suspected the evil origin of an illness. At times I practiced a short exorcism during confession when I was faced with particularly stubborn sin, such as homosexuality. Saint Alphonsus Liguori, Doctor of the Church for moral theology, told confessors that the priest, *before anything else,* must privately exorcise whenever he suspects demonic infestation.

A strict interpretation of the current *Ritual* allows the exorcist to intervene only if diabolic possession is suspected. All other instances of evil influence can be resolved through the normal means to obtain grace: prayer, the sacraments, sacramentals, group prayers for deliverance, etc. This is too wide a field to be abandoned to private initiative without any specific norm. In the Appendix to this chapter is the letter that the Congregation for the Doctrine of the Faith sent to all bishops on September 29, 1985. This letter reminds the bishops of the current norms, without addressing the complex problem that is facing the committee that is revising the *Ritual.* I do not know if bishops sent comments and suggestions to the said committee, but I doubt it very much, given the current lack of interest in the matter.

Cardinal Suenens is undoubtedly one of the most sensitive among bishops to the problems of exorcisms. He is most aware of the current reality because he lives it through the prayers of deliverance practiced by the renewal groups.

In his book, which I have already mentioned, he writes, "Deliverance from demons that is practiced without a mandate and without exorcisms begs problems of demarcation that must be addressed and resolved. At first glance, the borderline appears clear: when demonic possession is suspected, exorcisms are reserved exclusively to the bishop and those whom he delegates. Anything else is an open and nonregulated field, which therefore is accessible to everyone."

However, the cardinal knows full well that the instances of true possession are few and require a specific and expert diagnosis before they can be determined. Therefore, he adds, "Everything that is outside true possession is like a field whose boundaries are blurred and ill defined, where confusion and ambiguity reign. The very complexity of the terminology does not help to simplify matters; there are no common definitions, and we find many different problems under the same label" (*Rinnovamento e potenza delle tenebre*, p. 95).

In subsequent pages the cardinal offers practical suggestions: "It would be most useful if, among others, we could spell out the terminology and establish with clarity and precision the difference between *prayer of deliverance* and *exorcism of deliverance*, with emphasis on demons. The *exorcism of deliverance*, in case of possession, is reserved to the exclusive discernment of the bishop. Nevertheless, when it comes to exorcisms to be administered outside instances of complete possession, there is no clear borderline" (ibid., pp. 119–20). To be honest, I can see a clear line of demarcation according to the following criterion: a true exorcism, reserved to a bishop or his delegated agent, is a *sacramental*, and as such it pledges the intercession of the Church; all other exorcisms are a form of *pri-*

vate prayer, even when practiced by groups. I do not know why Cardinal Suenens did not speak of exorcism as a sacramental and as the only form of deliverance that can properly be called exorcism. Although he devotes a few chapters of his book to sacramentals and cites some examples, he does not list exorcism among them; in my opinion, including it among sacramentals would define it clearly, at least on this point. I am sure the Cardinal will forgive me this observation.

Cardinal Suenens has the following practical suggestions: "I suggest reserving to the bishop not only cases of demonic possession, in accordance with the old norms, but to give him jurisdiction over all instances of suspected demonic influence. Although the office of exorcist has disappeared, at least as one of the minor orders, any episcopal conference could ask Rome to reinstate it" (ibid., pp. 121–22). The Cardinal suggests allowing the laity to be granted the office of exorcist for less severe cases.

Father La Grua, in the excellent book that I have already cited, gives other suggestions. He mentions Cardinal Suenens' advice and adds some advice that could be followed in the interim, while waiting for official decisions. These suggestions are very practical and, if acted upon, could provide good material for the committee that is reviewing the section of the *Ritual* on exorcisms.

> In every diocese, the bishop should appoint a *discernment group*, of three or four individuals, to work side by side with each exorcist; each group should include a psychologist and a doctor. Every instance of *suspected* demonic activity should be brought to this group, who, after appropriate research, would refer the patient to the proper place: a doctor, an exorcist, or a prayer group. All lesser incidents should be referred to the prayer group, or groups, according to the need, and the exorcist would be referred only the most severe

occurrences. A priest should always be present in every prayer group.

Deliverance, therefore, should always be part of the *pastoral care for the sick*. A well-defined *therapy* should span the following: evangelization, sacramental practice of the sacraments of penance and the Eucharist, spiritual exercises, affiliation with prayer groups. Needless to say, in minor incidents, a prayer group would not be allowed to exorcise but only to pray over patients, unless an authorized priest were present (ibid., pp. 113–14).

Increasing the number of exorcists and training them to administer their ministry properly are not the only challenges. There are many other open questions that must be resolved before this will no longer be a chapter in the Church's book that is sealed with the sign "Work in progress". The devil never ceases his activity, while the Lord's servants *sleep*, as the parable of the wheat and the darnel tells us. The first step, the fundamental step, is to reawaken the awareness of bishops and priests, according to sound doctrine that Scripture, tradition, and the Magisterium have always transmitted, even through the Second Vatican Council, the teachings of the last popes, and lately the *Catechism of the Catholic Church*, which I have quoted in my earlier chapters. The principal purpose of my book is to contribute to this reawakening, and I will consider myself successful only if I reach this goal, regardless of any praise, critique, or large volume of sales.

Appendices

A Document from the Congregation for the Doctrine of the Faith

This is a letter that was sent to all the ordinaries of the world to remind them of the current guidelines regarding exorcisms. I do not know why some newspapers talked about "new restrictions". There are no novelties, but the final exhortation is important. The novelty may be included in the second paragraph, because it repeats that the faithful cannot use the exorcism of Pope Leo XIII, but the letter does not mention that priests need their bishop's permission. I am not sure whether this variable was intended by the Congregation. I have some doubts about the interpretation of paragraph 3. The letter is dated September 29, 1985. Here is my translation.

> For some years there has been an increase in the number of ecclesial gatherings which seek liberation from demonic influences, even though they are not properly and truly exorcisms. These groups, even when a priest is present, are led by lay persons.
>
> Since the Congregation of the Doctrine of the Faith has been asked what ought to be thought about this, this dicastry is of the opinion that all other ordinaries should have the following response:
>
> 1. Canon 1172 of the Code of Canon Law declares that no one is able to legitimately undertake exorcisms of the possessed unless expressed and individual permission has been obtained from the ordinary of the place (§ 1). The

canon also establishes that this permission ought to be conceded by the ordinary of the place only to priests who are distinguished by piety, knowledge, prudence, and integrity of life (§ 2). Bishops are, therefore, strongly urged to see to the observance of these norms.

2. From these prescriptions it follows, therefore, that no member of the Christian faithful can use the formula of exorcism against Satan and fallen angels, extracted from that which was made law by Leo XIII, and even less are they able to use the entire text for exorcism. Bishops are to bring this to the attention of the faithful as it is deemed necessary.

3. Finally, for these same reasons, bishops are asked to be vigilant that—for even cases in which a true diabolical possession is excluded, diabolical influence nevertheless seems in some way to be revealed—those who do not have the required faculty not serve in the leading of meetings where, in order to gain freedom, prayers are used which dignify demons by directly questioning them and in searching to make known their identity.

The announcement of these norms, however, ought not keep the faithful from praying that, as Jesus taught us, they might be delivered from evil (cf. Mt 6:13). Finally, pastors ought to avail themselves of this occasion to recall what the tradition of the Church teaches about the proper function of sacraments and the intercession of the Blessed Virgin Mary, the angels and the saints in the spiritual fight of Christians against evil spirits (Cong. Doctrine of the Faith, Sept. 29, 1985, letter to local ordinaries. Prot. no. 291/70; *AAS* 77 (1985): 1169–70; *EnchVat* 9, nn. 1663–67).

It Is Dangerous for the Amateur to Attack the Devil

The above-cited letter warns against any direct dealings with demons and states that their name should not be asked by those who have not been granted the specific faculty to do so. The Acts of the Apostles report a particularly fitting event:

And God did extraordinary miracles by the hands of Paul, so that handkerchiefs or aprons were carried away from his body to the sick, and diseases left them and the evil spirits came out of them. Then some of the itinerant Jewish exorcists undertook to pronounce the name of the Lord Jesus over those who had evil spirits, saying, "I adjure you by the Jesus whom Paul preaches." Seven sons of a Jewish high priest named Sçeva were doing this. But the evil spirit answered them, "Jesus I know, and Paul I know; but who are you?" And the man in whom the evil spirit was leaped on them, mastered all of them, and overpowered them, so that they fled out of that house naked and wounded. And this became known to all residents of Ephesus, both Jews and Greeks; and fear fell upon them all; and the name of the Lord Jesus was extolled. Many also of those who were now believers came, confessing and divulging their practices. And a number of those who practiced magic arts brought their books together and burned them in the sight of all; and they counted the value of them and found it came to fifty thousand pieces of silver. So the word of the Lord grew and prevailed mightily (Acts 19:11–20).

Besides the misfortune of the seven brothers, I want to point out that people converted and left the practice of magic (the cult of Satan) to embrace the word of the Lord (cult of God). This is very different from what happened once to Father Candido, who was performing this ministry under the authority of the Church. One day he was exorcising a strong woman, who was easily enraged, in the presence of a psychiatrist. Suddenly, the woman rose from her chair, clenched her hand in a fist, rotated around herself—as athletes do before throwing the discus with force—and hit the right temple of the exorcist with all her strength. The sound of the blow reverberated throughout the large sacristy, and the psychiatrist worriedly rushed toward the priest. Father Candido serenely continued the exorcism, smiling all the while, as was his custom. When the session was over, he said that he had felt as though a velvet glove had grazed his temple. Obviously, heaven had protected him in a manner that I do not hesitate to call extraordinary.

CONCLUSION

I have reached the end of my book, without saying anywhere near to all that I could have said. I wrote with the intent of turning the fruits of my direct experience into practical help for the faithful, because no other book in print today has done so. I hope that I have been of service to all who are interested in the topic of exorcism. I especially had my fellow priests in mind; all of them should have at least a basic, concrete knowledge of the subject, because they must be able to discern when there is an evil presence requiring an exorcist, or when an exorcism would be futile. I have already said this, but it bears repeating because it is most important.

I must thank Cardinal Poletti, who found me totally unprepared when he gave me this assignment, which I accepted blindly. Now I realize that this faculty, which was given to me without any merit on my part, is a completion of my presbyterial role; that is, just as I celebrate Mass, preach, and hear confessions, so too I exorcise when it is necessary. I am grateful for the possibility to help so many people who suffer and who often need only one word of understanding. At this point I would feel like half a priest if I did not have this ability, even if it is an exceptional form of priestly ministry that is a vital part of the ordinary ecclesiastic pastoral activity, or at least it should be.

I will also say that I have received great spiritual benefits from this ministry. Because I have, so to speak, touched with my own hands the invisible world, my faith has increased. Because I continually realize man's absolute impotence in the presence of these ills, my prayer life and my humility have received a boost; as much as we try to pray with devotion and commitment, we are truly "worthless servants". If the Lord does not take over, the fruits of our efforts and of the ability that we acquire through experience are zero. When I say *zero*, I am not exaggerating; it is Saint Paul who says, "God gave the growth" (1 Cor 3:6).

I also want to refute a popular belief that, I do not know how, has managed to convince a good portion of the clergy: that is, the conviction that the devil retaliates against exorcists. My teacher, Father Candido, who exorcised full-time for thirty-six years, suffered some physical illnesses due partly to age, but not to the devil. Father Pellegrino Ernetti, a Benedictine monk from Venice, exorcised for forty years, and this ministry neither improved nor worsened his health. I will continue to repeat this—and I beg you to believe me: the devil is already causing each one of us as much harm as he is allowed to do. It is false to believe that if I leave him alone, he will leave me alone. It is not only false; it is also a betrayal of our priestly ministry, which should be directed solely at leading souls to God, even by removing them from Satan's power, if necessary. To this end, evangelization is of primary importance, then the sacraments, and lastly, sacramentals, and exorcisms among them. A priest who is afraid of the devil's reprisal can be compared to a shepherd who is afraid of the wolf. It is a groundless fear.

It would be futile to overestimate any vengeance staged by the devil to discourage exorcists. These are rare instances, and I will mention one of them. One day a priest was helping Father Candido while he was exorcising a young man. During the session the clothes of the victim caught fire; nothing much happened, only a slight burn on his shoulder. The mother later told us that the undershirt also burned, but the young man did not suffer. However, during this incident, there was a sudden smell of sulphur, and the demon turned to the priest, threatening him with grave consequences.

A few nights later the priest was driving from Naples to Rome. Suddenly two lights approached him on his side; he could not figure out what was happening and decided to stop at a service station. While he was approaching the service area, his car caught on fire. The priest managed to stop, remove the keys, and escape. Other motorists ran toward the car, yelling, "There is someone in the car, there is someone in the car!" The priest could not convince them that he had been alone in the car. Suddenly the burning car's engine started, and the car began to move forward slowly, almost as a ball of fire, toward the gasoline pumps. At the same time, a strong smell of sulphur wafted through the air. The priest recognized the same scent he had smelled during the exorcism and began to pray. Immediately the car stopped but continued to burn until it was totally destroyed.

I mention this incident because I want to paint the entire picture, but it would be a generalization if we viewed this as a rule; it truly was an exception. Everyone knows that the priestly ministry includes risks and discomforts for the priest, even when he does not exorcise. Saint Peter would say, "Rejoice in so far as you share Christ's sufferings, that you may also rejoice and be glad when his glory is revealed" (1 Pet 4:13). The welfare of souls is worthy of every sacrifice.

The priest must believe in his priesthood; he must believe in the power the Lord gave him; he must walk in the footsteps of the apostles and of the holy priests before him. John XXIII, at the beginning of his papacy, reminded everyone of the Curé of Ars. It is true, the saint tore souls out of Satan's grasp, and he suffered much because of the devil. On the other hand, he was not an exorcist and did not exorcise anyone. It is the Lord who is in charge, and he never gives us greater trials than we can endure. Woe to us, however, if we back down through cowardice and abdicate our duties.

We have the gift of the Spirit, the Eucharist, the word of God, the power of the name of Jesus, the protection of the Blessed Virgin, the intercession of the angels and saints; is it not silly to fear the vanquished? I pray Mary Immaculate, enemy of Satan and victorious over him from the first annunciation of the Resurrection, to enlighten, protect, and sustain us all during our earthly battle until we reach the eternal reward. Particularly I pray for the Catholic bishops, who *are obligated* to take on the responsibility of all who suffer because of the devil; may they respond to the need, in accordance with the law and tradition of the Church.

Immaculate Mary! It gives me great consolation to finish thinking about her, who has a God-willed enmity against Satan: "I will put enmity between you and the woman" (Gen 3:15). She is *Immaculate* because she never was stained by original sin or by actual sin; that is, she never gave in to Satan. She is *always Virgin* because she always belonged to God, in body as well as in soul, and from her the Word received his Body. When we think of the value of the Incarnation, we are reminded of the devil, who has no body because he is pure spirit. In his great arrogance, he wanted to be the center of all creation; instead, after the Incarnation he was forced to realize that it is Christ who is the center of creation and that Christ is true God and true

Man. He is also forced to admit that the Incarnation also marked the beginning of his defeat. That is why he tries every trick to force man's body to become an occasion for sin. He tries to humiliate the body, to break it, as a raging reaction against the Incarnation of the Word, who, through his sacrificed Body, redeemed us. We can realize the importance of this Marian dogma: Mary ever Virgin, in opposition to Satan, is an instrument of the divine plan.

Mary declared herself the servant of the Lord, and she became the *Mother of God*, thus acquiring a unique intimacy with the Holy Trinity. We can imagine Satan's opposition to this event: he rejected God, and, by turning away from him, he became the creature most distant from him. It should make us realize the total failure of Satan, who, falling away from heavenly joy, plunged into eternal torment.

Mary, our *Mother, the Mother of the Church, the Mediatrix of all graces*, constantly shows us her dynamic works by the will of Christ, who chose to associate his Mother in his work of the sanctification of souls. She also shows us her decisive opposition to all of Satan's works, because they are directed against God's plan for man, and it is to this end that Satan persecutes us, tempts us in every possible way, and, not satisfied to be the root of all evil, sin, pain, and death, tries to drag us with him to eternal damnation.

Here I stop. After writing four books about Mary, I would not want to start with the fifth at this point, when it is time to draw to a close. The writer Manzoni warns us, with his usual common sense, that one book at a time is sufficient, and, at times, it is one too many.

PRAYERS OF DELIVERANCE

Prayer against Malefice
FROM THE GREEK RITUAL

Kyrie eleison. God, our Lord, King of ages, All-powerful and All-mighty, you who made everything and who transform everything simply by your will. You who in Babylon changed into dew the flames of the "seven-times hotter" furnace and protected and saved the three holy children. You are the doctor and the physician of our soul. You are the salvation of those who turn to you. We beseech you to make powerless, banish, and drive out every diabolic power, presence, and machination; every evil influence, malefice, or evil eye and all evil actions aimed against your servant . . . where there is envy and malice, give us an abundance of goodness, endurance, victory, and charity. O Lord, you who love man, we beg you to reach out your powerful hands and your most high and mighty arms and come to our aid. Help us, who are made in your image; send the angel of peace over us, to protect us body and soul. May he keep at bay and vanquish every evil power, every poison or malice invoked against us by corrupt and envious people. Then, under the protection of your authority may we sing, in gratitude, "The Lord is my salvation; whom should I fear? I will not fear evil because you are with me, my God, my strength, my powerful Lord, Lord of peace, Father of all ages."

Yes, Lord our God, be merciful to us, your image, and save your servant . . . from every threat or harm from the evil one, and protect him by raising him above all evil. We ask you this through the intercession of our Most Blessed, Glorious Lady, Mary ever Virgin, Mother of God, of the most splendid archangels and all your saints. Amen!"

Anima Christi

Soul of Christ, sanctify me; Body of Christ, save me; Blood of Christ, inebriate me; Water from the side of Christ, wash me; Passion of Christ, strengthen me; O good Jesus, hear me; within your wounds, hide me; let me never be separated from you; from the evil one, protect me; at the hour of my death, call me; and bid me come to you; that with your saints, I may praise you forever and ever. Amen.

Prayer against Every Evil

Spirit of our God, Father, Son, and Holy Spirit, Most Holy Trinity, Immaculate Virgin Mary, angels, archangels, and saints of heaven, descend upon me.

Please purify me, Lord, mold me, fill me with yourself, use me.

Banish all the forces of evil from me, destroy them, vanquish them, so that I can be healthy and do good deeds.

Banish from me all spells, witchcraft, black magic, malefice, ties, maledictions, and the evil eye; diabolic infestations, oppressions, possessions; all that is evil and sinful, jealousy, perfidy, envy; physical, psychological, moral, spiritual, diabolical ailments.

Burn all these evils in hell, that they may never again touch me or any other creature in the entire world.

I command and bid all the powers who molest me—by the power of God all powerful, in the name of Jesus Christ our Savior, through the intercession of the Immaculate Virgin Mary—to leave me forever, and to be consigned into the everlasting hell, where they will be bound by Saint Michael the archangel, Saint Gabriel, Saint Raphael, our guardian angels, and where they will be crushed under the heel of the Immaculate Virgin Mary.

Prayer for Inner Healing

Lord Jesus, you came to heal
our wounded and troubled hearts.
I beg you to heal the torments that
cause anxiety in my heart;
I beg you, in a particular way, to heal
all who are the cause of sin.
I beg you to come into my life
and heal me of the psychological harms
that struck me in my early years
and from the injuries that they caused
throughout my life.

Lord Jesus, you know my burdens.
I lay them all on your Good Shepherd's Heart.
I beseech you—by the merits of the great, open
wound in your heart—
to heal the small wounds that are in mine.
Heal the pain of my memories,
so that nothing that has happened to me

will cause me to remain in pain and anguish,
filled with anxiety.

Heal, O Lord,
all those wounds that have been
the cause of all the evil that is rooted in my life.
I want to forgive
all those who have offended me.
Look to those inner sores
that make me unable to forgive.
You who came to forgive the afflicted of heart,
please, heal my own heart.

Heal, my Lord Jesus, those intimate wounds
that cause me physical illness.
I offer you my heart.
Accept it, Lord, purify it and give me
the sentiments of your Divine Heart.
Help me to be meek and humble.

Heal me, O Lord,
from the pain caused by the death
of my loved ones, which is oppressing me.
Grant me to regain peace and joy
in the knowledge that you are the Resurrection
      and the Life.
Make me an authentic witness
to your Resurrection,
your victory over sin and death,
your living presence among us.
    Amen.

Prayer for Deliverance

My Lord, you are all powerful, you are God,
    you are Father.
We beg you through the intercession and help
of the archangels Michael, Raphael, and Gabriel
for the deliverance of our brothers and sisters
who are enslaved by the evil one.
All saints of heaven, come to our aid.

From anxiety, sadness and obsessions,
We beg you. *Free us, O Lord.*
From hatred, fornication, envy.
We beg you. *Free us, O Lord.*
From thoughts of jealousy, rage, and death.
We beg you. *Free us, O Lord.*
From every thought of suicide and abortion.
We beg you. *Free us, O Lord.*
From every form of sinful sexuality.
We beg you. *Free us, O Lord.*
From every division in our family, and every
    harmful friendship.
We beg you. *Free us, O Lord.*
From every sort of spell, malefice,
witchcraft, and every form of the occult.
We beg you. *Free us, O Lord.*

Lord, you who said, "I leave you peace, my peace I give
you", grant that, through the intercession of the Virgin
Mary, we may be liberated from every evil spell and
enjoy your peace always. In the name of Christ, our
Lord.   Amen.

ACKNOWLEDGMENTS

The Publisher gratefully acknowledges permission to reprint from the following published works:

St. Teresa of Avila: The Book of Her Life, from *The Collected Works of St. Teresa of Avila*, volume 1. Translated by Kieran Kavanaugh and Otilio Rodriguez. Copyright 1987 by the Washington Province of Discalced Carmelites. ICS Publications, 2131 Lincoln Road, N.E., Washington, D.C. 20002, USA. Used by permission.

In general, the Scripture quotations are from the Revised Standard Version of the Bible, copyright 1946, 1952, and 1957; Catholic Edition copyright 1965 and 1966 by the Division of Christian Education of the National Council of the Churches of Christ in the USA. Used by permission.